Copyright © 1!
13435 N.E. W
Phone (503)

Most of the paintings in the book have been shown on Public B₁
Workshop" Series 1. Call your local P.B.S. television station for information. It is my hope that this
book and the television series will help you better understand many of the different ways to approach
watercolor and encourage you to pick up a brush. Painting is so much fun and not only rewarding for
yourself but also bring for those that you give your paintings to. The fear of picking up a brush and
worry about making a mistake in class can be overwhelming but you can start to build your confidence
at home and you'll surprise yourself. Once you feel more comfortable local classes are so much fun
and you'll soon realize everyone was at sometime a beginner. Focus on your success and don't be too
hard on yourself as you gain.

I've had the great privilege of sharing my love of painting with so many people who thought
they couldn't paint but wanted to try. Start by trying some smaller versions of larger paintings on
greeting cards. I've found by doing several greeting cards you can try different color variations and
find the colors that are most appealing. You'll be able to share these paintings with friends and they will
be far more special than one you purchased. The most unsettling moment when you start is touching
the brush to the surface. Keep your sense of humor as you grow.

While I've shared ideas for paintings for you to follow, don't restrict yourself and be afraid of
making many changes. I'm sharing techniques in this book that I hope you'll be able to put to use in
many variations. I love to see photos of how you've made changes in your painting. I'll be glad to
return your shared photos and thank you for sharing them with me.

My family is the most important thing in my life. There constant support, love and help has
made my life so rich and full of joy and laughter. It's because of their love I am able to share my
love of painting. To my husband Stan, my daughters Camille and Kimberly, my mom Birdie and Joe
who all work with me and are an incredible help, thank you.

While I can't share my fabulous family, I can share my years of learning and teaching. While
often there are several ways to approach a painting, I've tried to explain easy to follow techniques
and instructions.

I've had the privilege of working with an outstanding staff that is like an extended family.
You can take classes from these talented, caring and sharing people. Write us for class information.

I hope the pages ahead will provide encouragement and positive reinforcement for you, your
family and friends. It is always such a pleasure to receive letters and cards from many of you who have
enjoyed painting.

GETTING ORGANIZED

It is so easy to set up an area for watercolor. I prefer to paint with daylight along with studio light. Getting all my equipment ready prior to starting my painting is so helpful. The portable painting board is so easy to set up and the angle is very helpful. It is far more difficult to paint on a flat surface. Place the palette in an easy to reach area. Have a roll of soft paper towels handy. Use either a water container which has separated wells or a couple jars of water. Have a clean jar for a quick clean rinse and one that you use for normal rinse (refill with clean water often). Place your brushes in an easy to reach area. Also within your reach place a spray bottle to wet your palette or surface, a sponge for painting texture or wiping a surface, scrap paper to test color, a comfortable chair and you are ready to paint. A little soft music in the background is a nice added mood set.

SUSAN SCHEEWE TUBE COLORS

Tube watercolor is my preference to use when painting. I feel I can achieve greater intensity and depth of color with tube colors, plus it makes it easier to cover large areas with pigment. Tube color has a moist paste consistency that you squeeze out onto the surface of the palette, once the color has been placed on the palette it will start to dry but can easily be re-wet for use again and again.

Martin/F. Weber manufactures tube colors under the Susan Scheewe line. Pigment rich, these creamy smooth watercolors are more concentrated that the more traditional transparent watercolors and are capable of a full range of tonal values from the deepest to the softest washes. The colors are lush, responsive, rich, intense and brilliant, capable of infinite variety and subtleties. Susan Scheewe watercolors were formulated not only for depth of color but also for there ability to capture a scope of subject matter. They are also versatile to accommodate a wide range of easy-to-master quick tricks and a variety of techniques with quality for success. While you can always dilute a color with water you can't strengthen the color and it's important at times to have good strength in color

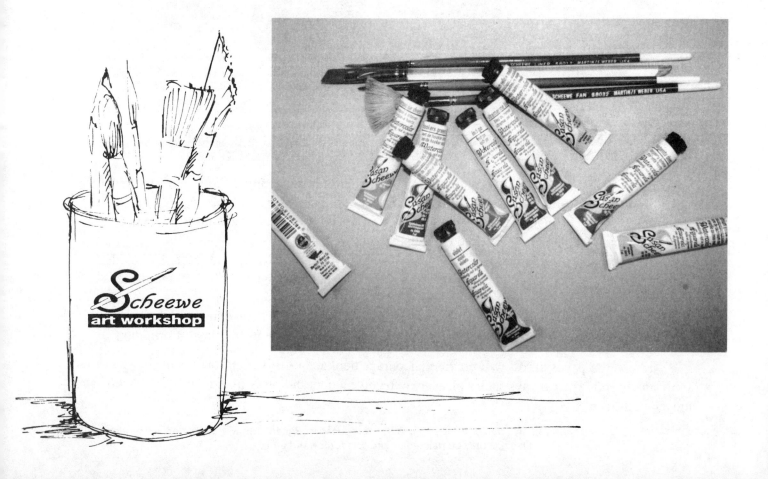

WATERCOLOR PALETTE

The Martin/F Weber Company asked me to design a palette that I would like for watercolors, what a privilege. While there are many palettes already on the market I felt designing a palette with many separate color compartments for mixing and keeping colors fresh would be most helpful. Throughout the years of teaching, I have watched students who had palettes with large open, mixing areas which result in muddy colors. I wanted to help eliminate this problem.

The Martin/F Weber Company made a plastic watercolor palette that is designed to keep colors clean while including areas for mixing in wells. The 28 wells were designed to meet the needs of various painting styles. There are three styles of wells within the palette. The angled wells are used by placing the paint at the top of the well, and then mixing in the recess, this gives you precise mixing control. In the round wells around the outside edge I place pure pigment, it is easier to maintain the pigment in a pure working manner.

In the deep wells it is easy to mix large amounts of color for larger applications of paint. These can be easily rinsed at the end of the day.

The clear lid enables convenient travel and storage of the palette. When storing the paint, use the lid to guard against dust and foreign particles from getting into the paint. The lid can also be used for an additional mixing area.

For easy clean up, take a paper towel to absorb excess water or pigment. Secure the lid. When you want to resume painting, just refresh the dried colors with a brush or mist over the palette with a spray bottle.

PALETTE LAYOUT

It is far easier to establish a fixed location for each color on your palette with the colors you most often use. It's important to be consistent so you can find your colors when you want them. I prefer lining up warm colors on one side and cool colors on the opposite side. I place blues and greens in the large mixing areas as I use more of this pigment in either large sky washes or in foliage areas.

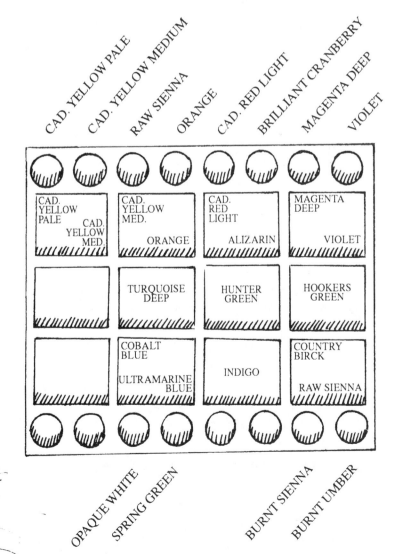

GETTING ORGANIZED

PORTABLE TRAVEL BOARD

I love this portable travel board. It is the easiest way to support your paper while you work. The surface has been finished for easy clean up and can be wiped with a paper towel. The clips on the back fold out to give an excellent angle for working. The top clips can hold the sheet, a photo or a sketch for painting reference. Depending on the type of paper, you can easily tape the paper to the surface on all edges or just secure the top edge for heavier papers. The handle at the top makes it easy to carry when painting in different locations.

PAPER TOWELS

Have a large amount of soft paper towels handy while you paint. It is important to keep clean ones close by because you could pick up paint from a dirty paper towel that will appear on your paper where you don't want it.

RESIST STICK

The wax resist stick is applied to areas of a painting where you want the watercolor pigment to repel the surface. You can vary the appearance according to the amount of pressure used to apply the wax and the surface texture. This can be a fun technique to use on rough paper as the wax tends to stay on the peaks. The smooth hot pressed paper can almost block the surface completely.

The resist can be applied to the paper to create sparkle, texture and highlights. You can apply this to the surface before you start to paint or over

light washes that have been applied. Plan ahead, you could get resist where you don't want it and the pigment will not go over the top.

This is an excellent tool to keep handy to put the sparkle in water.

SPRAY BOTTLES

I use two different types of spray bottles while painting. I have a larger spray bottle which contains clean water. I use this larger spray bottle to dampen my palette prior to painting and as I continue to paint to keep my pigment a nice workable consistency. I can also use this to dampen my paper before I apply paint when using a wet-in-wet technique.

I use the smaller spray bottles for travel keeping one with clean water. Play with filling a spray bottle with color, mix only about 1/4 or 1/2 of the small bottle. Keep test paper handy to check the color and distance you may wish to hold the sprayer for a certain effect. Have fun and experiment with several color mixtures. You will soon discover the many beautiful textures and applications possible.

MIXING PIGMENTS

When you add water to your pigments, the value will become lighter in appearance the more water you add. It is far easier when painting to build diluted glazes rather than trying to lift out dark pigment off the paper surface.

MIXED MEDIA

While not traditional, watercolors can be mixed with other water soluble media such as acrylics. Experiment on small greeting cards before you try mixing mediums on a larger painting. I use a disposable palette designed for acrylics. Don't use your acrylics in plastic palettes, the pigment can dry hard and be extremely difficult to remove if at all.

There are many wonderful variations you can use along with watercolors such as pen and ink, modeling paste, watercolor pencils, and gouache. You may want to combine watercolor pencil texture with your watercolors

TAPE

Tape has long been used as a painting aid while doing watercolor. Tape was available far before friskit came along.

It is important that you have fresh tape. Tape can become too sticky when it is old and could tear the surface. Tape is also sensitive to the heat and should not be sat in an area where the sun beats down on the roll.

Tape can be used to preserve the white or can be applied over a dry wash. Since papers vary in softness it's best to test the tape on an area before you apply it to the surface of a large sheet. Once the tape has been applied to the surface, don't use a hair dryer on it since this could adhere it to the paper.

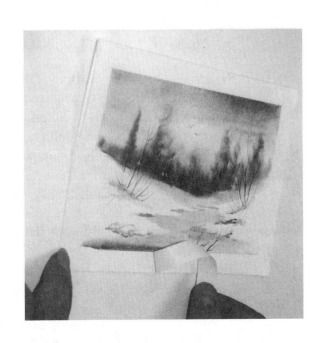

WATERCOLOR PAPER

Watercolor papers come in a variety of types and weights. While there are many variations they can be divided into three groups; cold pressed, hot pressed and rough. There are variations within these groups by weight and texture. The weight is expressed in pounds referring to the weight of a ream of 500 sheets, not to the weight of an individual sheet. The most common sheet size is 22" x 30". Papers can be purchased by the sheet or in a variety of smaller sizes in pads and blocks

Watermarks do not come on all papers, but when they do it indicates the side you'll select to paint on. Hold the paper up and you'll be able see if there is a watermark in the lower corner section of the sheet.

Cold-pressed is the most popular and has a slight texture that holds the paint well but does not interfere when painting details.

Hot-pressed is smooth and lends itself to pen and ink with watercolor washes or fine detail and linework.

Rough paper has a lot of texture. The pigment settles in the lower section which adds to the textured appearance of some subjects. It is often overworked due to the texture and it is difficult to achieve the detail that is far easier to paint on the cold or hot-pressed.

Lightweight papers tend to buckle when wet. I prefer at least 140 lb. cold pressed for large paintings as I don't want to fight buckles or take the time to stretch the surface.

Try several papers and you'll quickly discover some work better for your technique than others. Keep a notebook and place scraps of these papers in a plastic sleeve, write on these papers what you liked or didn't like about the performance. Be sure to write the brand and weight on the paper as these variations are of great importance.

COLOR CHARTS

It's very important to make color charts if you are just starting to paint with watercolors. Cut 8 x 10 sheets of watercolor paper that you will later place in plastic sleeves for a reference notebook.

Label the brand, color and type of paper you test the colors on. Start with strong pigment and dilute it as you work across the sheet with water show gradation of color. The sheets become a valuable reference.

STRETCHING PAPER

If you are getting a lot of buckling out of the type of paper you've selected it would be wise to stretch the paper. Tack the paper down using brown packing tape around the outside edge then wet the paper. If you are on a wooden surface you can staple the pre-wet paper. The paper will still buckle the first time you wet it, but as it drys it will flatten back down if it is secured to the board. If the paper has serious problems with buckling you might consider a heavier watercolor paper.

SALTING

Fascinating effects can be achieved by *LIGHTLY* scattering salt crystals in wet paint. Salt works in watercolor because it repels the pigment while attracting moisture. Each grain of salt you drop creates a spot. You will find some colors stain the paper and hardly lift while others work wonderfully. Paper also makes a great deal of difference as well as the dampness of the paper and the type of salt used.

The salt absorbs the paint creating light uneven spots. Experiment with the salt. It can appear as snowflakes, small flowers in a bouquet or the appearance of texture in a background. Most often the wetter the wash, the larger and fainter the shape will be. Once the surface becomes dry, salt will not affect the surface.

Try different kinds of salt for variations in effect. Try the large rock salt and then try Margarita salt. I most always use table salt.

SALTING continued

A common mistake is placing too much salt on the paper the first time. Give a few minutes for the salt to dissolve in the pigment. Don't use a hair dryer as it would push the salt around. Natural drying time gives the best results. Allow the surface to dry completely before you brush off salt.

Make several different 8 x 10 sheets using different papers and colors for your reference notebook.

ERASING

You can remove unwanted transfer marks using a soft PE-1 eraser. Don't rub really hard while using an eraser, as you could damage the surface. Most often the eraser on the end of a pencil is too hard and could also damage the surface. Never erase while the paper is damp as it is very easy to damage the surface.

Once the painting has completely dried, you could come back and very lightly remove graphite lines you've missed. Leaving a few pencil lines is fine but if they bother you - take them off carefully.

TERMS

WASHES

Washes are diluted applications of paint. A graded wash is a wash which makes smooth transitions from light to dark values. Flat tone washes are even value and color. A wash laid on dampened paper has a soft diffused quality. Applying a wash to dry paper requires much faster work.

PRE-WET

A term used for wetting an area of paper with clean water before applying any paint. This process will allow you to blend your colors easier, and work the paint longer on the paper. I use this often as I prefer the working time it allows me as I apply color.

WET-IN-WET

A process of adding paint into a wet area that already has been either pre-wet with clean water, or using a brush with both pigment and water.

The blending or diffusion of color in the wet area depends upon the amount of water and paint in your brush when applying it to the paper surface. There is always the potential for backruns if the paper isn't evenly wet . To avoid backruns don't leave puddles of water. Some artists soak the paper completely before painting. I most often pre-wet sections.

BLENDING

A gradual transition from one color or tone to another. The gradation of color is far easier to achieve when working wet into wet so the colors flow into one another. To avoid a hard edge from being formed, quickly apply clean water at the edge of the last stroke.

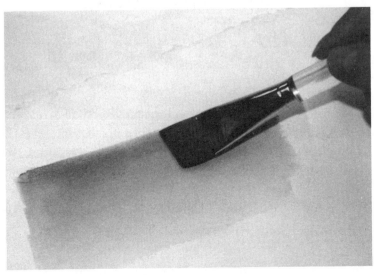

DRY BRUSH

This technique is just what the name implies - using a brush that is almost dry. The almost dry brush will skip across the surface of the paper so the color partially covers the paper. This is very helpful in creating the appearance of texture.

Be careful to dilute the paint a little while the brush is slightly damp, you do not want to apply straight pigment. Practice on a sheet of scrap paper, too much water and pigment will make a blob and too little or dry doesn't work well either. Make sure the underpainting is dry or the colors will diffuse.

SPONGES

Sponges are wonderful for mopping up unwanted paint or moisture. For quick clean up, it's a great tool! Sponges are also helpful for applying the appearance of texture or applying flat large washes.

Dabbing the paint onto the paper with a sponge gives an attractive mottled effect. With the many varieties of sponges, it's nice to have several sizes and shapes to create special effects. Small natural sponges are excellent to create the appearance of foliage or dab on a rock shape.

You'll find that sponges come in a variety of sizes, shapes and textures. The wool sponge has a lot more holes which create wonderful foliage, while the silk sponge has a far less textured surface. The photo shows the wool sponge in use.

Sponges are also useful to wet backgrounds. As you wet the surface be careful not to rub or scrub hard and damage the paper.

Keep a clean sponge handy and ready to use when painting. Be sure to wash thoroughly when you have completed the painting.

SPLATTERING

The flicking of paint onto the paper can create the appearance of rocks on a bank, sand on the beach, snow, spray in a waterfall, to name a few ideas. Spattering often adds the appearance of texture, creating more depth in a painting. Practice on scrap paper to see how diluted you want your paint.

SCRATCHING

You may want to scratch into wet paper to create twigs, grass, distant trees, or birds. When you scratch with the handle of the brush this may be a creative technique. Practice on scrap paper to see the many effects you can achieve.

ACCIDENTAL SCRATCHING

The paper can be damaged prior to painting by an accidental scratch with a ring or sharp object. This can create a problem in your finished painting. Be sure to check your paper prior to starting. The paper in a scratched area pulls more pigment and will make a dark appearing line.

BLOOM

Bloom, backrun, watermark or flower are all words that describe the appearance of a mark or area that dries unevenly on the paper. It is a personal thing if you like this appearance or not, some painters do these deliberately. They are most often caused by placing a very wet brush into a damp area which moves the pigment creating the watermark or bloom. To avoid this try to work wet into the freshly wet area or wait until the surface has completely dried and then continue on. Always wipe off excess water on your brush before picking up paint.

If you start to get a backrun, act quickly and try to even the moisture on the surface. You can lift off some of the excess pigment with a dry brush.

FOLIAGE BRUSH TAP

Prior to starting your painting, place the angular bristle brush in your water container for five minutes. The water will cause the brush to flare, making it very easy to create a small dot pattern. Lightly tap the brush against the paper to create the light texture of the foliage. This brush is easy to control when lightly tapping to create shapes.

The foliage brush can take on a different appearance by adding more water to the brush. This is especially helpful in the first applications of color. Allow the first application to dry, then build up layers of pigment with repeated applications.

DRYING

The drying time can be affected by paper, pigment, temperature, humidity and air circulation. All sorts of elements can affect the drying time.

Should you live in a very high humidity area, you will want to watch that mold does not grow in standing watercolor palettes. Should mold appear, wash the entire palette, wipe and wash with Pine Sol, then rinse and start again.

Should you live in a very dry area and the paint is drying so fast you can hardly handle it, add a few drops of glycerin in the water.

SPRAYING

Having a fine mist spray bottle is a very handy item. Often after the paint has set on the palette overnight, I'll spray it with water prior to starting my painting.

A spray bottle with clear water is also handy to mist a background. Be careful not to have a heavy sprayer as it could result in uneven water drops.

LIFTING OUT

Removing paint from the paper can be a very helpful painting technique. You could pat a wet sky area with a sponge, soft paper towel or brush to create clouds. You can lift off pigment with a brush to create veins on a leaf. You'll think of many ways you can use this technique.

Should an area dry darker than you planned, you can dampen the area and blot with a dry paper towel to lift the paint. Some colors are more difficult to lift out because they stain the paper, such as Sap Green. If you plan to lift out colors, try them on test paper first. You'll also find some papers make it very difficult to lift off color.

HARD AND SOFT EDGE

This is just what it sounds like. Rather than having hard line areas along an edge, you can dampen to create a blending or soft edge. Using both hard and soft edges gives a more realistic appearance when painting as well as being very eye appealing.

TEXTURE MEDIUM

WHAT MAKES IT DIFFERENT THAN MODELING PASTE?

The texture medium was made to a whiter and creamer consistency than modeling paste. The creamer consistency will allow ease for the user to apply a design with a brush. The white formulation will allow delicate transparent watercolor or acrylic washes to appear bright.

The modeling paste is an excellent medium as well but designed for heavier application, most often applied with a painting knife for large dimension on canvas or wood surfaces.

WHAT IS THE DRYING TIME?

The drying time depends on several variations:
1. How much water was added on the brush.
2. Humidity and temperature.
3. The surface which it has been applied.

DOES THIS WORK LIKE GESSO?

No, it's designed to build texture. Gesso would crack with this much texture applied.

DOES THIS SHRINK?

Yes, there is some shrinkage but minimal.

CAN YOU ONLY USE THIS ON WATERCOLOR PAPER?

This product can be used on wood, tin, plastic or glass. While it can be used on metal, it should not be put on a mailbox as the expansion and contraction over time of the metal would create a problem.

CAN YOU USE OTHER TYPES OF PAINT WITH THIS MEDIUM?

Yes, it can be painted over with not only watercolor but acrylic or oil.

SHOULD YOU PUT THIS ON A SUE SCHEEWE PALETTE?

No the medium would be difficult to remove once dried.

CAN YOU MIX PIGMENT INTO THE MEDIUM?

Yes, either watercolors or acrylic can be used to mix and color tint the medium. Once the watercolors have been mixed into the medium they become permanent and won't move as a traditional watercolor.

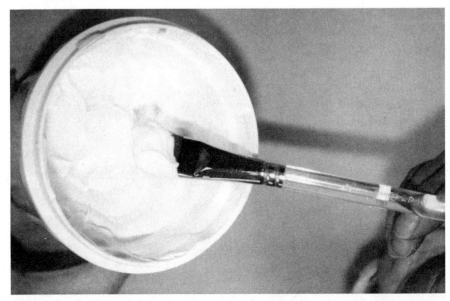

BRUSHES

Excellent quality brushes are extremely important to your painting results. The brushes I use are the Sue Scheewe signature brushes, manufactured by Martin/F Weber Co..These wonderful brushes are designed to execute the many different watercolor techniques with ease. Thirty years of teaching and painting was brought into the design and selection of these superior brushes.

Please note that each series number is a different configuration of brush (the handle as well as the hairs). In each series there is several sizes of brushes available. The size of the brush you use, depends on the size of the painting.

The brushes can be used for watercolors and acrylics as well as for oil. *However*, once they have been used with oils, mark on the handle with a permanent marker the word oil. These brushes should then be kept for use only with oils. I have a set of these brushes for oil use. It is extremely helpful to have a couple of your favorite brushes in the same size and series so you will always have a clean brush ready to apply fresh color. While these brushes have great strength and durability, they will wear with harsh use and need occasional replacement as any brush would.

ANGULAR SHADER

This is one of my very favorite brush series. The shape allows so many possibilities and ease of painting. When loading only the point of the brush with pigment it is easy to achieve a beautiful gradation in color. The brush can be turned or twisted to fit into small spots as well as with larger areas. We should never use just one brush but if I had to this would be the brush.

ROUND

The round brushes should have a taper that comes to a sharp point. These are excellent for painting details. These create beautiful flower petals on daisies, graceful tree trunks and branches. They can also be used to wash in large areas. The rounds are capable of a stroke which varies from thin to thick appearance. This is a very traditional brush.

LINER

The liner is excellent for creating continuous lines without running out of paint. The pigment flow smoothly down the fibers making it easy to paint small details.

FILBERT

With a twist of the wrist this brush makes beautiful flower petals and ribbon shapes. The chiseled edge is wonderful for drawing lines.

FLAT

These excellent flat brushes taper to a sharp point. The flats are fantastic for laying in a wash.

BACKGROUND ANGULAR

This is a wonderful brush to lay in backgrounds. The angular configuration makes it extremely easy to cut in around flower shapes.

FAN BRISTLE

The bristle fan makes it easy to pull up and create grass and foliage. Tapping the brush up and down lightly can create the appearance of tree foliage.

FAN SYNTHETIC

This is a great brush for creating delicate hairs in animals. Sweep the brush lightly and make a grained appearance on wood textures.

FOLIAGE BRUSH

This is an angular bristle brush that is wonderful for creating foliage. Place the brush in the water for a few minutes prior to use, if you are just starting your painting. The water will fill the bristles, making the brush flair. Tap off the excess water on a paper towel, dip it in to the pigment, then on a test sheet of paper, check for color and the amount of water in the brush. If the brush is too wet, the color will blob together. If the brush is too dry, almost no pigment will come off. With a little practice this will fast become one of your favorite brushes.

You'll soon discover you can use several colors on the brush at once to create variations in foliage areas.

Foliage Brush

Background Angular

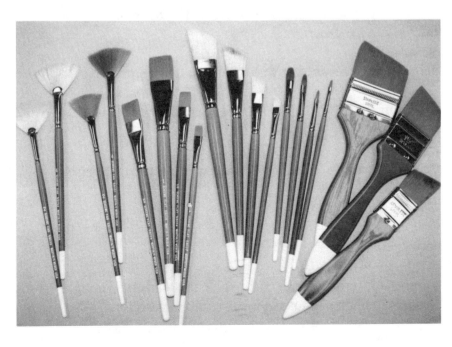

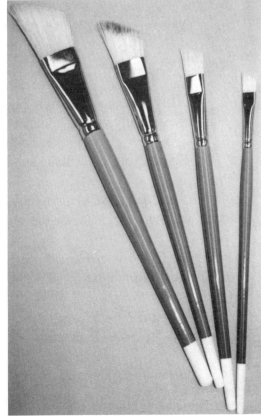

HELPFUL HINTS

I've found while teaching, some areas that could be helpful as you learn more about watercolor. I've learned many of these helpful hints over the years usually by making a mistake and then learning from my mistake. I hope these hints will help you avoid some possible problems.

Make yourself a reference notebook. This notebook can be full of plastic sleeves containing color charts, tests using salt, special effects you've tried, sketches, and different papers that you can refer to for future projects. Your notebook can be a wonderful source of material you have used, and knowledge you have gained. Include brush technique samples and special colors you've discovered that work well together.

Protect your paper prior to use. Be very careful not to damage the surface by accidentally scratching the surface with your fingernails, bracelet or painting knives. Don't store your paper where items could come in contact to scratch the surface. Be extra careful around the family cat, it could accidentally damage the surface with it's claws.

Don't place hand lotion or oil on your hands prior to handling the paper surface. This could create areas that repel the water.

Graphite papers can be helpful but many can create a problem due to the oil or wax in the paper. I prefer Saral, as it works well for transferring my designs. Pencil can be used; allowing the pencil line to remain is permissible in watercolors. Removal of these lines can be done with a soft eraser. You may not find transfer paper available in your area. An alternative is to rub a soft graphite pencil on the backside of tracing paper and then transfer to the surface.

Pencil erasers are most often too hard and can damage the paper surface. Use a soft white eraser or gum eraser to remove unwanted lines.

Watercolors dry lighter than they appear when wet. There are several factors in how light a watercolor will dry, depending on the pigment, water and paper. As a good rule always go lighter and deepen the color slowly.

ALWAYS start with light pigment and deepen slowly as you will create far less problems for yourself, especially with pigments that tend to stain the paper.

Should you accidentally splatter paint, immediately blot it with a clean soft towel or sponge.

Should you use a hair dryer to speed drying time, BE CAREFUL not to turn it on full blast next to the painting as it can cause the wet paint to move.

Be fair to yourself and use at least 140 lb. paper. It is easier to use a cold press paper verses using a hot or rough paper.

When making greeting cards, buy the envelopes first and cut the paper to fit. Cards are fun to paint and a great way to practice your painting.

If sending a postcard, remember to protect it from the elements. You can do this by putting a coat of spray varnish over the painting. You would normally not use varnish on a watercolor.

Be careful not to over scrub the paper. Over scrubbing a paper could damage the surface. Using a good 140 lb. paper will forgive some scrubbing, some of the more soft delicate papers can ball up.

Whatever you buy, the most important consideration is quality. The difference between poor brushes and paper and good material is the difference of making a painting a struggle or fun.

Keep a scrap of paper to test colors and occasionally a technique. Often you can save the test paper, add some notes and add it to your reference notebook.

Remember, when following instructions from the book; *IT IS YOUR PAINTING* so if you want to deepen, lighten or change colors you should do so. Color reproductions in paint rarely appear exact to the original painting. Even when I do the same painting twice they rarely turn out the same.

Should you accidentally forget to put the cap back on the watercolor tube and it has dried hard, cut the tube open. The paint is still good when dry, it only needs to be re-wet with water.

CLEAN UP

WASHING BRUSHES

Take a few minutes when you have completed your paintings at the end of the day and thoroughly rinse your brushes in clear water. Some colors will stain white bristles but this will not effect your paintings. Washing the brushes with a mild soap will lighten the stained appearance but, they will never appear the same as when they were purchased. Should they become bent, run the brush under hot water and then along the edge of an envelope, the glue on the envelope is water soluble and will help shape the brush again. Rinse the brush well before using if you have applied glue to shape them up.

BRUSH STORAGE

Place brushes in a jar or glass until they are completely dry. Make sure they don't press up against anything.

If you are using sables or other natural hair brushes you might add some moth balls if you do not foresee painting with them for some time.

COLOR CARE

After you apply paint onto the palette, wipe the top of the tube with a damp paper towel to clean away any traces of paint that would dry and make it hard to remove the cap when you use it again. Clean the cap as well if there are paint on the edges. Squeeze the paint from the bottom of the tube so you don't waste paint and suck in a lot of air that could cause the paint to dry some in the tube. Don't leave the caps off for a long period of time.

Should the tube cap become stuck try placing a match at the neck for a minute, be careful as the top will be hot and give it a turn.

If you find the paint has dried in the tube, as a last resort, cut open the tube and put the pigment on a palette. In my many years of painting this has only happened a couple times. There is nothing more frustrating than wrestling a little tube for a small amount of paint.

PAINTING SURFACE

Clean your drawing board. Paint that has been left on a board could dissolve and work its way back onto fresh paper during your next painting. I like the travel board as the finish is easy to clean . A wood board can absorb pigment and appears messy.

PAPER CARE

Watercolor paper should be stored with care. Store the paper in a flat area or in a portfolio. Keep paper away from moist areas. Be careful not to have hand lotion on your hands when handling paper, the grease can cause the pigment to resist the surface at a later time when painting.

CLEAN PALETTE

Clean or wipe the palette to remove splatters at the end of the painting day, you might need to stop and wipe the areas back some in mixing areas as you paint. While it is not necessary to wipe off the clean colors as you can simply wet them when you paint another day. It is very important to clean the palette when colors become muddy.

The Scheewe palette has a plastic lid to protect the pigment from gathering dust or foreign particles. You can also use the lid for an additional surface for mixing colors.

SUNFLOWERS
"COUNTRY FLAVORS"
PAGES 28 - 31

DELICATE IRIS
PAGES 22-27

CHILDREN PAINTING

What a wonderful gift to give to a child. Paints, paper and brushes were my favorite gift.

Buy them good brushes, paint and paper. Guide them in how to take care of the brushes. I started painting at a very young age as did my children. These are the most special paintings.

While trying to guide children encourage them as they grow and don't become too critical or they become frustrated. Ask them about the painting. I have found with young children their spirit is so great and they aren't afraid. The children that paint learn an awareness of colors in our life that are so beautiful in landscapes, flowers and just everything they touch.

Greeting cards are such a special gift when done by the hands of a child. Use the watercolor paper cards or make them from watercolor sheets. They can be framed and will become a wonderful memory as the years pass by.

Children love to see their paintings framed and hung on display for all to enjoy. You can also take there are work and have calendars made very inexpensively. How much fun it is to make these calendars for family members and friend. Kinko outlets make these as well as many fast print color shops.

Halloween and Thanksgiving cards and invitations hand painted will soon become a treasured keepsake.

Scrapes of paper become wonderful gift tags.

Rainy days soon fill with sunshine when the paints come out to fill the hours. Be sure the precious works of are signed and dated.

MAKE A NOTEBOOK

Make yourself a reference notebook. A three ring standard notebook with plastic sleeves will become a wonderful reference source. I have many notebooks I have made and I use them often.

Start the notebook with color charts. Make at least 5 sheets so you can separate yellows, reds, blues, greens and grays. Cut the paper to fit inside the plastic sleeves. Start the swatch of color with pure pigment and dilute with water as you brush across the surface. The gradation in value can be a great reference source. Write the color and brand of the pigment used.

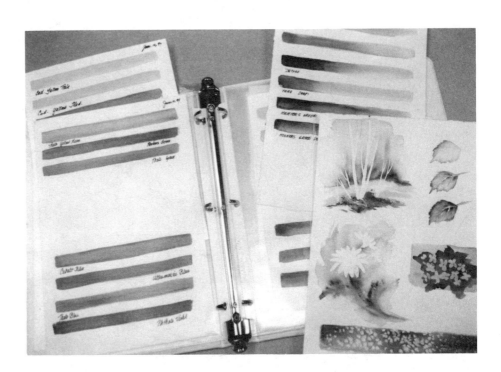

Watercolor Notebook
Example of sleeves
in the notebook.

*Texture Medium can add
yet another dimension to
these elegant flowers.*

©1994 Scheewe
Brown

DELICATE IRIS

SUSAN SCHEEWE WATERCOLOR
Cobalt Blue
Deep Magenta
Violet
Brilliant Cranberry
Hookers Green Deep
Hunters Green

BRUSHES
Series S8010 1/2 Inch Angular Shader
Series S8017 Size 1 Liner

Greeting Card
140 lb. Cold Press Paper

The beautiful delicate iris are always a favorite to paint. On the PBS Series I painted the iris on a plate using Permalba acrylics. You should use acrylics when painting plates because watercolor will not wash well. The acrylic can be wiped with a soft cloth but is still for decoration and not for use in a dishwasher. You could also paint several greeting cards with different variations of color. Keep a record of the colors you most prefer when making changes. Make a notebook for yourself and slip the card in a plastic sleeves for reference on another day.

The delicate iris are much easier to paint than they might first appear. I've included a big design that is fun to paint and would be perfect to try the many variations of elegant colors these flowers grow. You could easily make this on a large card for Mother's Day or a special birthday wish. You could send the card along with a mat for framing.

If possible, it is wonderful to have some fresh cut iris to paint from. Make a sketch of your own or transfer the painting guide.

If you have had your pigment on your palette for awhile or are just starting to paint, spray your palette with water.

Most often when I paint florals I start with the flowers. This keeps the flower colors bright and fresh, then I paint the background. The delicate bright flowers stay crisp allowing the bright surface of the paper to shine through.

UPPER PETALS

Pre-wet each petal with clean water, one petal at a time. Be sure not to pre-wet and paint two petals which are side by side at the same time. This will cause the colors to bleed into one another. You must wait for one petal to dry before starting the petal next to it. Use the angular brush picking up more pigment on the point of the brush. Place color to the outside edge of the petal and pull towards the center forming the contour. There are so many varieties that some have a real ruffled edge while some are only slightly ruffled. Shading is really important. Don't get rushed with your colors. If you aren't sure of the color you want, paint one on a test sheet and hold it near your surface.

FLOWER BEARDS

The beards should be painted before the flower petals for safety sake. Apply a little Cadmium Yellow Pale and Cadmium Yellow Medium tapping up and down on the beard. Then come back and tap a shadow on the lower section of the beard using the round brush.

IRIS LOWER PETALS

The same rule applies as with the upper petals; alternate painting the petals to avoid the bleeding of colors. Pre-wet the entire petal prior to applying color. Pick up the paint on the point of the brush and place the point on the edge of the petal, concentration color on the edge. Be aware of where the curl or turn back ruffles are located.

If the petals dry lighter than you desired, allow the paper to dry and then pre-wet with clean water and apply another glaze of color. Tap up and down under the beard with a a darker glaze for shadowing.

BACKGROUND

Pre-wet the entire background with a 1 or 1-1/2 inch background brush and clean water. Keep in mind it is always easier to start light and work darker. Sweep the leaf shapes on the wet surface so the colors diffuse nicely. If the paper starts to dry, re-wet the surface. Use diluted Hookers Green and Hunters Green with a dash of Violet. Use the angular brush and twist it as you pull to form the illusion of very distant leaf shapes. While you are allowing this area to dry, paint the center area between the two top petals.

LEAVES

Use the angular shader to develop the leaf shapes. Slowly layer on glazes of diluted Hunters Green and Hookers Green. As you add additional layers, apply hints of Cobalt Blue and Violet. Put a hint of the flower color into the shadow areas.

FINISHING

Use the chisel edge of the angular or a liner to pull out veins onto the petals. Use the flower color, making sure you watch the contour. If you make them too deep in value or too straight they will appear stiff.

Paint several greeting cards trying a variety of colors.

Receiving a hand painted card from a loved one is extra special.

*Follow the instructions for Delicate Iris
to paint this pattern.*

Pattern is continued on the following pages.

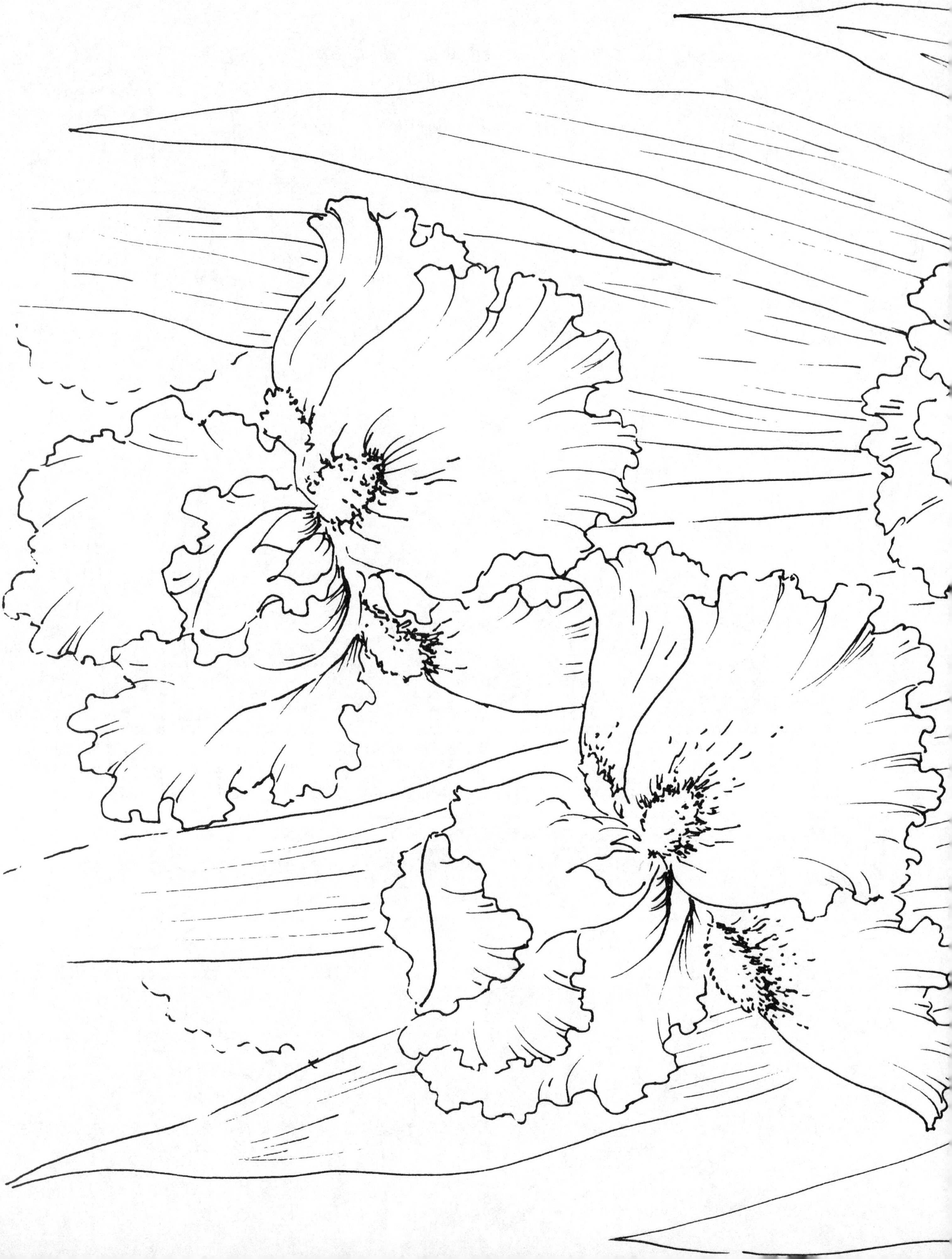

The paper you select can make a great difference in the ease of painting and your results. You'll discover some papers are far more forgiving then others.

Before I painted these flowers, I picked several iris from our yard to use as models.

It is wonderful to paint looking at these delicate blooms as you paint.

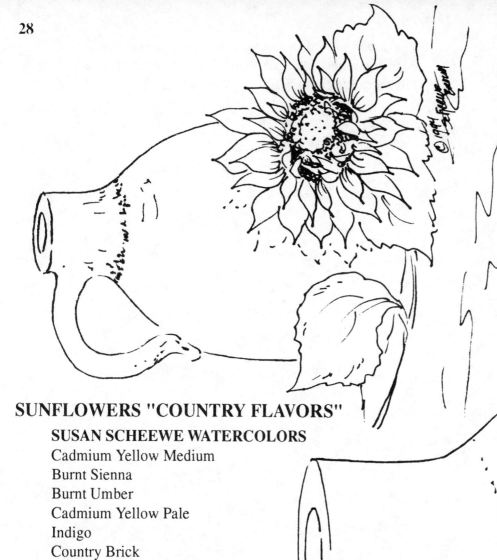

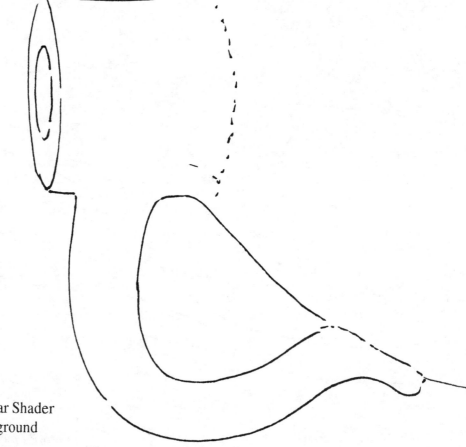

SUNFLOWERS "COUNTRY FLAVORS"

SUSAN SCHEEWE WATERCOLORS
Cadmium Yellow Medium
Burnt Sienna
Burnt Umber
Cadmium Yellow Pale
Indigo
Country Brick
Hookers Green
Hunters Green
Raw Sienna
Orange

BRUSHES
Series S8010, 1/2 Inch Angular Shader
Series S8012 or 13, 3/3 or 1 Inch Angular Shader
Series S8028, 1-1/2 Inch Angular Background

Natural Sea Sponge
140 lb Cold Pressed
Spray Bottle

Bring some sunshine into your home. Sunflowers are so very popular in home decor and fun to paint. You may want to do a design much like mine or change the container design by painting a crock or item you have in your own home or studio. It is important to have the freedom to rearrange, and adjust to your own personal taste.

We found this lovely old jug in an antique store on the east coat and I carried it home on the plane. It brings back found memories of the wonderful day we had just going into charming shops.

Transfer the painting guide to your surface or transfer a sketch for have made. You may want to make a sketch using a soft pencil directly on your surface. It's fun to have a couple of greeting cards ready to practice on and check a possible color variations to get them ready to paint.

Before you start take your spray bottle and dampen the colors on your palette. You may need to re-dampen the palette as you paint with a little spray of clean water.

JUG

Pre-wet the jug with a 3/4 or 1 inch brush going around the flower petals and the leaves. Make sure that you apply enough water for the paper to have a shine. While the surface is still has a shine pick up a mixture of Burnt Umber and Burnt Sienna on the 3/4 or 1/2 inch angular shader and start applying color on the left side of the container. As you work towards the right side dilute the mixture with water to lighten the value. Don't over work the colors on your palette but allow them to mix and mingle on your paper. Refer to the photo as a guide for color placement.

Now for some fun, use a natural sea sponge to create texture and an elegant old mottled appearance. Dampen the sponge and squeeze out excess water, pick up variations of pigment on your sponge using Burnt Umber, Indigo, hint of Burnt Sienna and for those who like a warmer appearance try a little Country Brick. Pat the sponge in the pigment and then on the damp surface. It's easy to control the amount of paint you apply by the pressure you use as you tap against the surface. If the surface or palette starts to dry, don't forget to use that sprayer to dampen either areas.

Paint patted on with a natural sea sponge will depend on the variety of shape and size. The silk sponge has a far finer texture than the wool sponge. I use both types depending on how much texture I want.

You will find the sponge a wonderful painting tool. Think of the many textures you can create on backgrounds, rocks and tree foliage. You could almost create an entire painting with sponges.

Next there are some areas that are just difficult to reach with a large sponge so you will want to use your brush in these small areas. On the lower left corner under the leaf apply color with the brush and then dab up and down with the corners of the brush.

In the photo you see a cast shadow but wait until you have painted the flower to apply this step.

SUNFLOWER

Use a 1/2 inch angular brush and pre-wet the entire sunflower with clean water. Next you are going to apply the first wash of color to work as a foundation for the petals. Paint all the flower petals using Cadmium Yellow Pale, this is a wonderful bright yellow. Form the petal shape with some care. Don't worry if pigment gets into the center area. Allow this area to start drying as you base in the center.

If the petals are really wet the center color will diffuse back from the center towards the outside edge, so make sure they are damp or dry. On the point of the 1/2 angular shader pick up more Burnt Umber and Burnt Sienna and apply to the center area. Dab the brush up and down to create a slight textured appearance or pat the center with a sponge. Apply deeper value around the outside edge of the center.

Pat the center area with a clean damp sponge or brush to lighten if the values become too dark. You can always go back and add more color.

While the petals and center area are drying work on the foundation for the leaves and will come back to these areas.

LEAVES

Start with the leaf shape on the far left. It is easier for the color to diffuse if you pre-wet the leaf using the 1/2 inch angular. Apply diluted mixtures of Hookers Green Deep and Hunters Green. A few touches of Cadmium Yellow Pale is nice.

Pick up less diluted, purer pigment on the point of the brush to add a few darker values.

As you paint the leaves near the flowers, still dilute the pigment but deepen the values next to the flower. Allow this foundation to dry while you go back to add detail to the petals.

SUNFLOWER GLAZING

Make each petal distinguishable by slowly adding deeper values to the petals. Using the 1/2 inch angular pick up a hint of Raw Sienna on the point of the brush. Apply the pigment on the lower petals. Should the color become too harsh rinse the brush and blend lightly with a clean damp brush. Slowly add additional color using hints of Burnt Sienna and Burnt Umber on the tip of the brush. Add hints of Cadmium Yellow Medium and Orange if you want a deeper colored flower.

The flower center can now be deepened around some of the petals. Don't make an adjustment if you don't feel it is necessary. You may want to lift out a little pigment to form a ridge. The centers can vary so greatly on each flower depending on the variety of sunflower and stage of development. I've bought sunflowers that have very dark centers and others which are far lighter with yellow and green tones. It's your painting so test those colors on the centers of your greeting cards.

CAST SHADOW

The sunflowers and leaves cast a shadow on the jug. Before you start think about the petal shapes you created when you apply the cast shadow. Use the angular shader with Burnt Umber and Burnt Sienna, and a hint of blue or violet is a nice option for cast shadows.

LEAF VEINS

Work back into the leaves with glazes one at a time. The vein is created by allowing a thin line of underpainting to show through as you apply pigment on each side.

GROUND

The ground area should be pre-wet with the 1-1/2 inch background brush. Apply mixtures of Burnt Umber and Indigo on the pre-wet surface. Dab with a sponge for a little texture. Deepen the value nearest the flower and the container.

JUG

At the top of the jug there is an area that should be painted deeper to make it appear as though there is a hole at the top to pour liquid from. Apply a mixture of Burnt Umber and hint of Indigo. Blot with a clean towel if it's too dark.

FINISH

Stand back and see if you need to add a few additional cast shadows.

Mats can make such a difference in the appearance of all paintings, select color that will accent the painting and room you plan to hang this spot of sunshine.

FALLS HARVEST

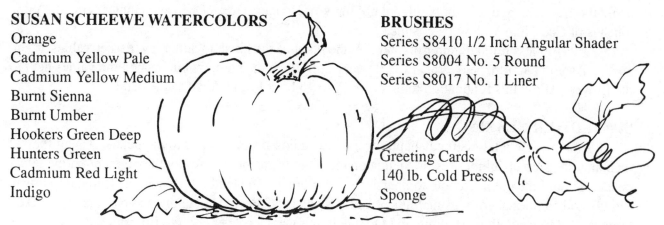

SUSAN SCHEEWE WATERCOLORS
Orange
Cadmium Yellow Pale
Cadmium Yellow Medium
Burnt Sienna
Burnt Umber
Hookers Green Deep
Hunters Green
Cadmium Red Light
Indigo

BRUSHES
Series S8410 1/2 Inch Angular Shader
Series S8004 No. 5 Round
Series S8017 No. 1 Liner

Greeting Cards
140 lb. Cold Press
Sponge

As with all paintings, this can be done in a variety of sizes. This can be painted on a greeting card to invite friends to a party or just used as a special note to friends and family during the Fall season. It is an excellent design for a child. The card will soon become a treasured keepsake by family and friends and can be matted and framed. We often focus on how well our own painting must appear and forget how special it is to receive a hand painted gift from someone we love.

The large painting could be used as a centerpiece for a Halloween party or Thanksgiving. Protect the surface by wrapping or covering it with plastic. Have your friends and family members who come for the special occasion write on the backside of the painting, being sure to include the date and year of that special time together. Be sure to include the younger children as you sign the back, as the years go past it will become a wonderful memory of a special time.

This is an easy painting to sketch using a pencil or transfer with graphite paper. You can have fun making all sorts of pumpkin shapes. Vary the size of the pumkins by the size of the brushes.

PUMPKIN

Pre-wet the entire pumpkin shape you have drawn. Go around leaves and the stem area. Use a 1/2 inch angular brush. Before you start to apply pigment, think of where you will place the highlight. Don't apply pigment in the highlight area, instead allow the paper to show through. Apply Cadmium Yellow Medium and Orange, this is the first wash, you will apply additional glazes. The yellow on the first wash will make the orange appear richer on additional washes. Be careful of the brush direction as you develop the sections of the pumpkins. Deepen the value as you paint the sides of the pumpkin.

The glazes will make painting the separations of the sections easy to achieve. The more glazes, the deeper the value will appear. Apply more Orange pigment on the left side. The light on the painting is slightly to the right. At this point you'll have a large pumpkin shape, but not a lot of definition. Leave this section and come back to work on it later.

LEAVES

You want to begin by putting a foundation on the leaves. The first step is thinking about light, dark and formation. Start using a 1/2 or 3/4 inch brush with diluted Hookers Green Deep and Hunters Green. A hint of diluted Cadmium Yellow Medium and Burnt Sienna is nice. This will serve as a base or foundation for continued layers. A hint of Spring Green is nice. Pick up the paint at the point of the brush. Then put the point of the brush down on the outside edge of the leaf so the color is stronger there. Pick up more water on the brush and dilute the color in the center area. For a more festive appearance on greeting cards, you could add on the leaf some of the Permalba Acrylic Gold diluted in a wash or add it at the edge of the painting.

LEAVES (Continued)

After the first wash has been applied, come back and add deeper values. Refer to the photo for a guide. Continue to build layers. Most often the underside of the leaves are lighter. Apply more pigment on the point of the brush for nice gradation of color. Now you can let this set for a little while.

GROUND AREA

Using a 1 inch or 1-1/2 inch background brush pre-wet the ground area. The pre-wet surface will allow the colors to diffuse out beautifully. Apply mostly Burnt Umber and Burnt Sienna with hints of Indigo. While this area is wet, tap up and down with a wool sponge. The wool sponge will create a wonderful texture. Come back with deeper pigment and apply under the pumpkin, leaves and vein with your angular shader. You can lift or add more color with this sponge. You'll find you can easily extend the background with this sponge.

You may need to lift out color with a clean damp brush in the area for the vein in the ground area.

PUMPKIN GLAZES

It's fun to see the rich colors created as you add more washes. You may wish to apply more Cadmium Yellow Medium or Orange. Pick up a hint of Country Brick, Burnt Sienna and a tiny touch of Burnt Umber, apply to deepen and separate the sections of the pumpkin. Deepen the area to the right and into the center or around the stem area. Be careful not to overblend this area as it will get a flat appearance.

LEAF GLAZES

As a general rule, the leaves that fall behind are deeper in value. By placing more green pigment on the point of the brush, you can deepen their color. Adding a hint of Indigo will help.

LEAF VEINS

You add so much richness and depth as you continue to build values. Don't put paint on the vein area, but paint on both sides of the vein. Placing a hint of pigment on the point of the angular brush and paint on both sides of the base color will make them appear lighter. Refer to the photo for a guide.

Paint a few leaves on the outside of an envelope and splatter with fall colors.

Paint a thank you card or hostess card to take with some apple cider or pumpkin bread to your friend.

Mats change the appearance of the finished painting.

Try several colors to find your favorite.

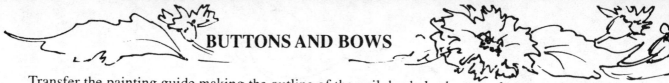

Transfer the painting guide making the outline of the pail, bachelor buttons, leaves and a light sketch of heather.

This is a fun painting to complete. It is easy to make many variations. When painting greeting cards it is easier not to add the bachelor buttons.

This painting includes several techniques - wet in wet, wet into dry, sponging, opaque touches and lifting out color.

Keep the sponge handy to lift off excess water. The damp sponge can be used to soften edges. You can also apply pigment to tap on color.

HEATHER

Pre-wet the top section with clean water, apply the water far beyond the flower shapes going over the top section of the container as well. The surface should be wet enough to shine. Should the paper start to dry, apply more clean water. Using a 1/2 inch foliage brush, tap the brush in Violet, Magenta Deep and a hint of Ultramarine Blue. Tap some excess water out on your paper towel as you don't want a flood of water, but it should be wet. At the same time check the amount of pigment you have picked up on the test paper. As you apply the pigment think of the flower shapes and try to avoid getting too much where you plan to paint the bachelor buttons and a few of the leaf shapes. The first application of pigment should appear light and the wet surface will create a soft diffused appearance. You will want to come back and apply additional pigment to deepen the flowers to the left, and lightly on the flower shapes to the right to create form. Lightly tap up and down with the foliage brush starting on the left. If you start on the left the flowers are deeper in value and the pigment will be coming off the brush and as you work towards the flowers on the right, they should appear lighter. Be careful as they will grow in shape as the water diffuses out. As the paper surface starts to dry you will get a more defined shape. If it starts to dry faster than you can paint, re-wet the paper with more clean water. You can go back and add a few more taps of color to deepen the shape but you'd want to wait until the surface becomes drier to give a little more definition and adjust the color.

BACHELOR BUTTONS

There will be a little diffused color from the heather that will show through the area behind the bachelor buttons. If the pigment is to dark where the heather has been painted, wet with a brush and blot to remove some of the color.

Use a 3/8 angular shader to apply the first wash of color to the bachelor button. Keep test paper handy as you work to test the colors. These flowers are painted in steps. The paper should be dry as you apply paint to the surface. Pick up more pigment on the point of the brush using variations of Ultramarine Blue, a hint of Violet and just a tiny touch here and there of Turquoise Deep. Start with a really light application of pigment keeping the point of the brush to the outside edge of the flowers. Allow a little of the white paper to remain on the full flowers or go back with a clean brush and lift out color in the centers. You'll want to apply several variations of diluted color as you move the brush around to create the ragged edge. You may want to add a few touches of color with the point of the round brush while creating this flower shape.

Using the round brush, tap in the centers using a deep mixture of Violet and Ultramarine Blue. With a clean damp brush dab up and down to soften the value and appearance at the top edge of the center.

On the lower sections of the full flowers, apply a medium value with just a few hints of deeper value to form the appearance of the inside of the petals. Pick up just a little pigment on the point of the round brush using variations of Violet, Ultramarine Blue and hint of Turquoise Deep, pulling in a few touches of Magenta Deep.

FALL HARVEST
PAGES 32-35

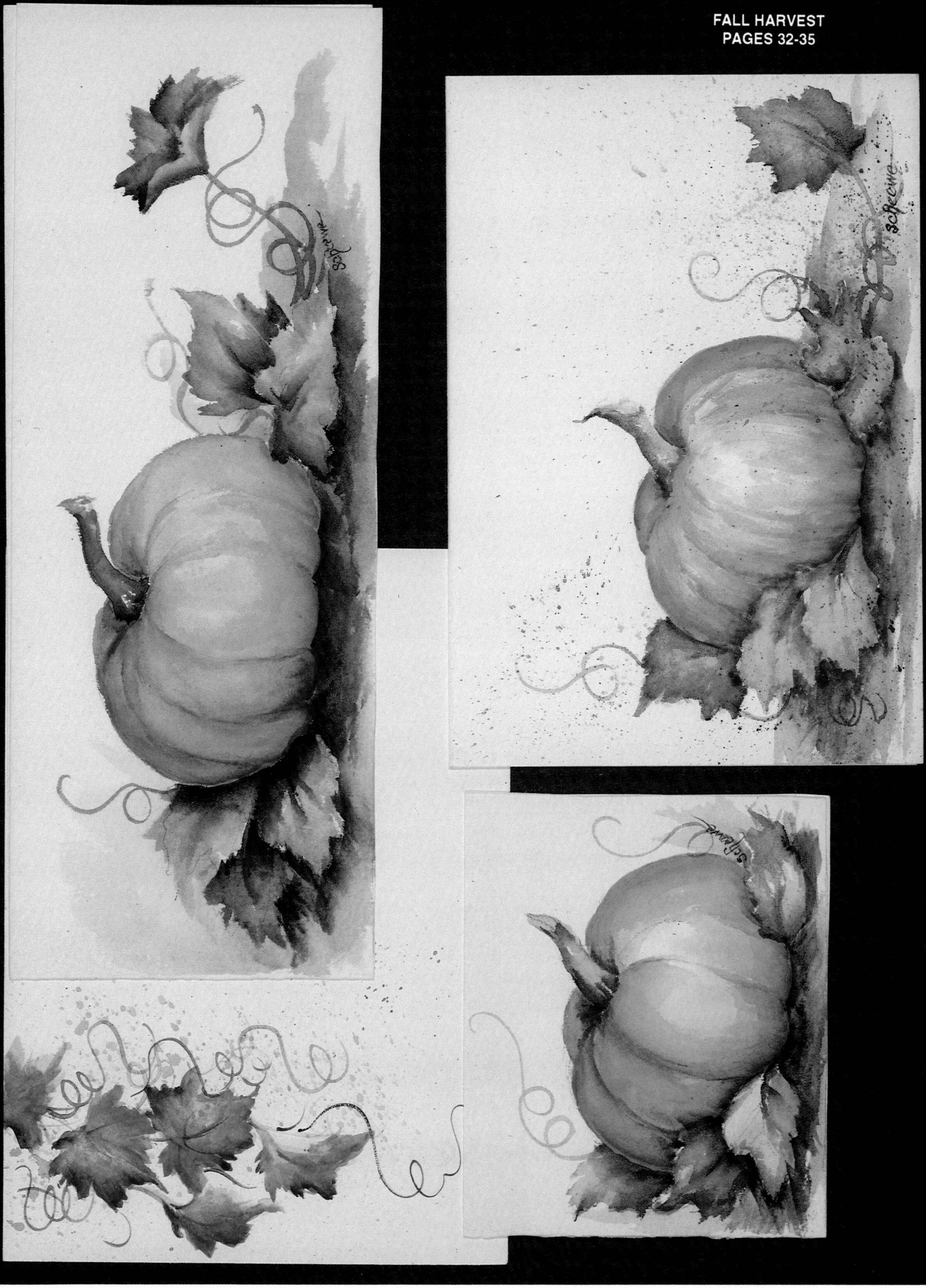

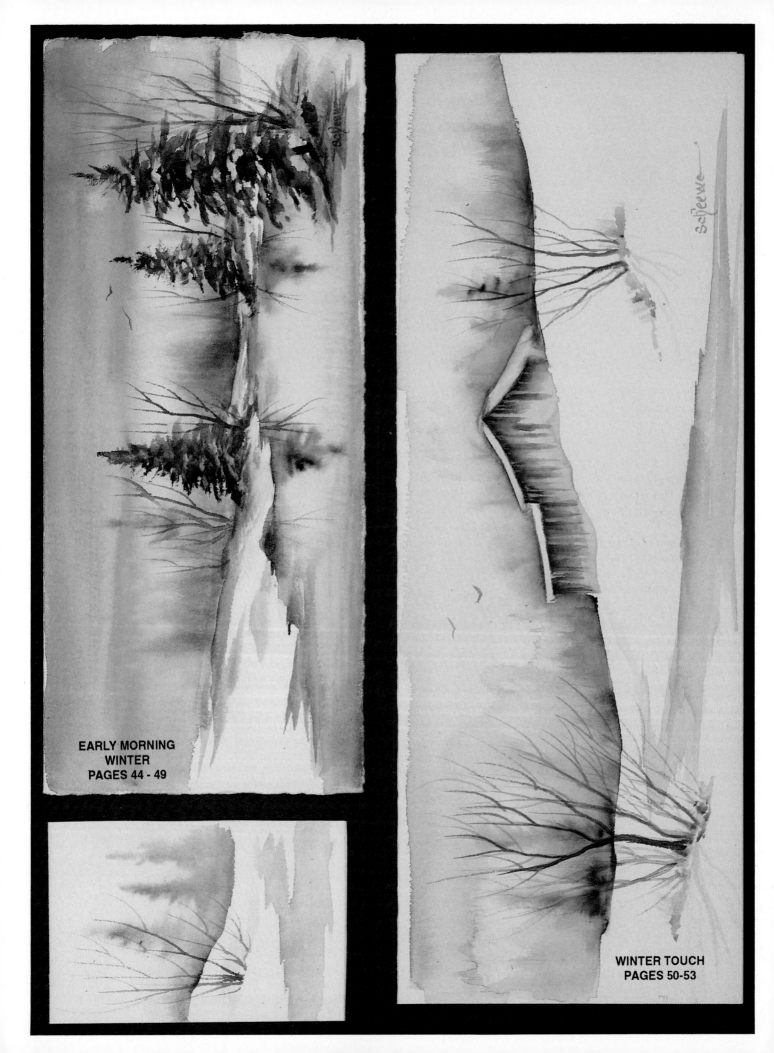

EARLY MORNING
WINTER
PAGES 44 - 49

WINTER TOUCH
PAGES 50-53

**EARLY MORNING
WINTER
PAGES 44-49**

WINTER TOUCH
PAGES 50 - 53

CONTAINER

Pre-wet the container with clean water using the 1 inch brush. Don't be afraid to get some water on the heather shape. While the surface is wet apply variations of Ultramarine Blue, a hint of Violet, and Magenta Deep. Using the 3/8 inch brush apply the diluted pigment to create form by having a slightly deeper value towards the left. With a damp sponge dab into a little of each color variation and tap up and down.

LEAVES

Start with the leaves at the top while you wait for the container to dry. Use diluted mixtures of Hookers Green Deep, Hunters Green and hints of Violet. Apply the pigment with the round or the chisel edge of the angular shader.

Apply deeper values on the leaves near the flowers.

STEMS

Apply the leaf color to the stems of the flowers using a liner or very little pressure on the point of a round brush. Deepen the value towards the left.

RIBBON

Use the liner to paint the ribbon. Pick the color you most like, some suggestions that work are blue, lavender, magenta or a mixture. Vary the pressure slightly as you pull the brush.

TABLE

Pre-wet the table area using the 1 inch brush. Be sure to come up a little along the sides of the container. Pick up a lot of Violet, hints of Magenta Deep, and Ultramarine Blue on the point of the 1 inch angular, start by placing the point of the brush on the left side of the container pulling across to the right. Brush the deeper values on the left of the container.

FINISHING TOUCHES

Once the painting has completely dried you may want to make a few adjustments. Moving the painting in a daylight area or to a darker artificial light can change the appearance. You can easily come back to the painting and deepen a value.

Should you discover you need a few touches of highlight on the bachelor buttons, you can use a little Opaque White. You may choose to use Opaque White alone or use a mixture of Opaque White with a hint of Ultramarine Blue. Just don't get carried away with the white, it can be a real aid when you've lost area that needs to be light and lifting color hasn't worked.

Why not paint several greeting cards using this technique. If you teach, these cards make wonderful examples of the many color variations you can paint. How fun to have cards ready to send to a friend or place on a gift.

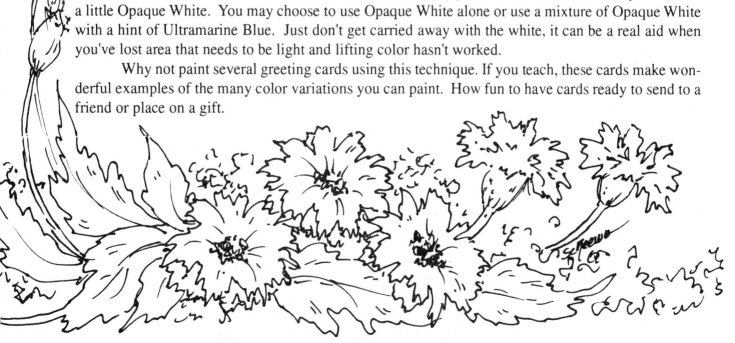

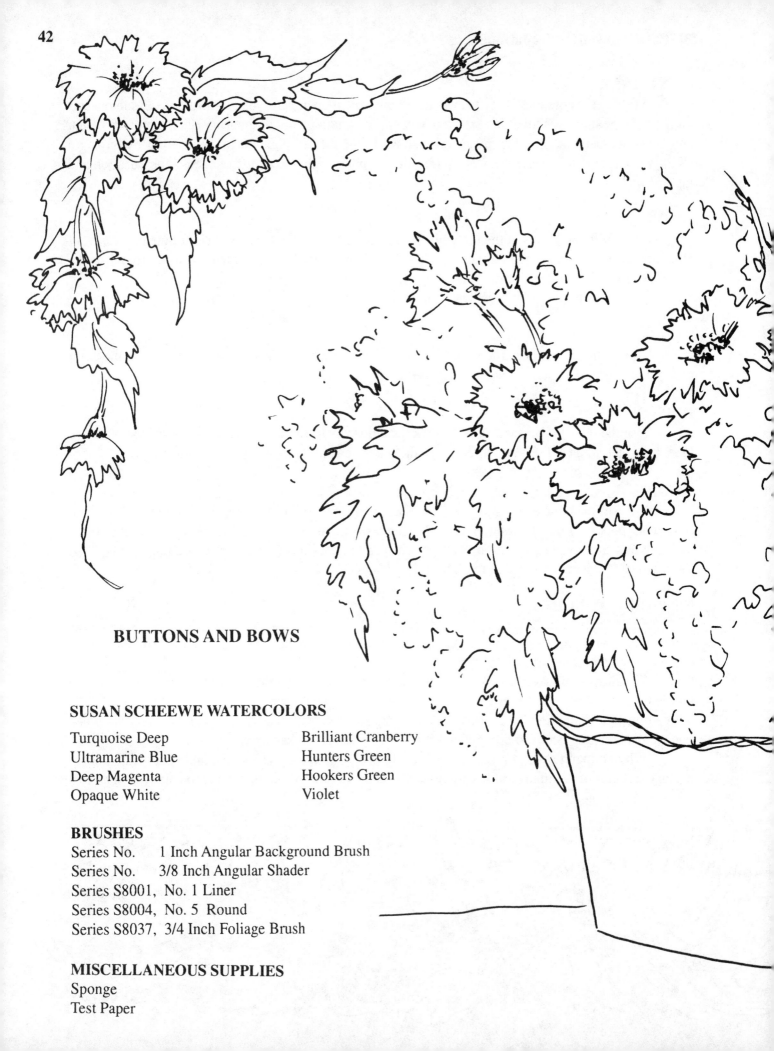

BUTTONS AND BOWS

SUSAN SCHEEWE WATERCOLORS

Turquoise Deep
Ultramarine Blue
Deep Magenta
Opaque White

Brilliant Cranberry
Hunters Green
Hookers Green
Violet

BRUSHES
Series No.   1 Inch Angular Background Brush
Series No.   3/8 Inch Angular Shader
Series S8001, No. 1 Liner
Series S8004, No. 5 Round
Series S8037, 3/4 Inch Foliage Brush

MISCELLANEOUS SUPPLIES
Sponge
Test Paper

Mats change the appearance of
the finished painting.

Try several colors to find
your favorite.

EARLY WINTER MORNING

SUSAN SCHEEWE WATERCOLOR
Cadmium Yellow Pale
Cadmium Yellow Medium
Cadmium Orange
Brilliant Cranberry
Magenta Deep
Violet
Hookers Green Deep
Indigo
Burnt Umber
Burnt Sienna
Cobalt Blue
Ultramarine Blue

BRUSHES
Series S8028, 1-1/2 Background Angular
Series S8010, Angular Shader
Series S8005, Size 5 Round
Series S8017, Liner Size 1
Series S8037, Foliage Brush 3/4 Inch
Series S8033, Fan Size 2

140 or 300 lb. Cold Pressed
Sponge
Spray Bottle

As a fun variation, add some texture medium to the top of the foreground fir trees, branches and on top of the rocks.

You can tint the medium by adding Cobalt Blue and Violet.

This is a quiet, beautiful scene.

EARLY WINTER MORNING continued

Did you ever look at those beautiful, brilliant morning colors just as the sun starts to rise over the horizon and wish you could do a painting to capture the beauty? It's my hope you'll enjoy this painting of an early winter morning and learn how you can also capture this in many other paintings you have designed. Have fun making a few greeting cards practicing this same technique before you start your larger painting.

Transfer the painting guide or make a sketch with a graphite pencil.

Spray your paints so they become moist and easy to pick up color.

Read all the directions before you start to paint.

SKY

Pre-wet the entire sky area, down to the ground line, using a 1-1/2 inch background brush with a lot of water. You want to make sure your paper has a shine before you pick up pigment. As you apply the pigment you can create either a brilliant striking color or dilute the pigments to create a softer appearance. Remember, this is your painting. The reason for pre-wetting this is so the colors will diffuse beautifully.

Use a 1 inch or 1-1/2 inch brush and pick up a little Cadmium Yellow Pale and Cadmium Yellow Medium. Apply long horizontal strokes, starting at the horizon line and working about half the way up the sky. Pick up a hint of water on the brush to dilute the color, if it appears too bright, wipe the surface with a wet sponge. Work fairly quickly as you paint the sky, spray lightly to re-wet or apply more water if the surface starts to dry. Next apply Cadmium Orange in long horizontal strokes lightly blending into the yellow and upward towards the top third of the paper. Continue towards the top of the sky, add both water and Brilliant Cranberry brushing across and blending to create a soft gradation of color. If you don't over blend you'll create not only a gradation but a soft cloud appearance. You may want to quickly dampen your palette with a spray bottle, using clean water.

Now you can come in and lightly tap on some clouds. If you love color you could use diluted Violet or Magenta Deep to apply clouds. If the clouds appear too dark quickly pat this with a soft paper towel to lift off color.

Quickly go to the distant trees while the sky is wet. If that area is dry, re-wet the area above the horizon with clean water.

DISTANT TREES

Quickly tap on distant trees as the wet surface will help diffuse them into the background and help create a hazy atmosphere. As the paper dries, you will get a more defined shape. Dilute the pigment to lighten with water. Pick up variations of mixtures of Indigo, Hookers Green and Hunters Green, apply more pigment towards the point of the brush. Make an interesting horizon line creating a few curves and gentle hills rather than pulling the brush straight across. Place the point of the brush towards the horizon pulling across and lightly tap upwards. Check your color frequently on scrap paper.

Come back while this area is still damp and apply a little more color using the 3/4 or 1 inch angular. Tap lightly up and down as you give these trees a little more definition of shape. As you tap on trees, think about making variations in size, shape and spacing. Be very careful you don't accidentally get them all alike. You can always come back and add a few more trees and you can dab the surface with a soft towel to lift off color.

WATER

Because water is transparent, it gets all its color from it's surroundings, either from objects seen through it or those reflected in it. Most often the sky has a great effect on the color.

Pre-wet the entire water area with clean water. Make sure you have a shine on the paper before you start. Use the 1-1/2 inch background angular or the 1 inch angular. When doing greeting cards, be sure to drop the size of the brush.

Be careful not to make a circle shape, instead make a far more interesting water line by creating an irregular water line.

Go up to your palette and pick up a little Cadmium Yellow Pale and Cadmium Yellow Medium. Come back to the surface of the paper and apply this mixture starting next to the distant bank. Allow the pigment to diffuse downward, if you are working on a flat surface, pick your paper up to help allow the pigment to run down. Allow for gradation of colors. Now pick up a little orange and blend slightly into the yellow and while brushing in a horizontal direction come down toward the lower section of the water. Rinse your brush and pick up Brilliant Cranberry, apply at the lower section of the paper and work horizontally as you work up into the orange application of pigment. You may want to add cloud colors if you painted them in the sky, using a mixture of Magenta Deep and Violet. You can always re-wet this area once it is dry and add more color.

TREE REFLECTIONS

Usually you can apply tree reflections after you have painted the trees. Another method is first drawing the tree trunk lines faintly where you would like them for placement and then tap a little reflection in the water. Use a 1 or 1/2 inch angular brush and pick up a mixture of Hookers Green Deep with a little Indigo and Hunters Green. Brush along the distant bank area and directly under the reflection cast from the trunk line. Tap up and down with the brush to form the tree shape and then rinse and wipe the brush and very gently wipe across in a horizontal direction. Keeping the paper at an angle will help allow the pigment to flow downward and diffuse into the wet surface. Be careful not to overwork this area. You can always let this dry and then dampen with clean water and apply more pigment.

GROUND AREA

You'll want to put some color in the ground. An easy way to keep continuity of color is to pull some of the colors from the bottom edge of the distant trees. Dampen the color along the bottom of the distant tree line with a clean brush and pull some of the pigment down into the snow area creating contours. Add a few touches of a diluted mixture of Indigo and Ultramarine Blue and apply hints of shadows at the distant tree line which should diffuse into the dampened area. Rinse and dampen the edge of color if a line if forming. Apply a hint of diluted Cadmium Yellow Medium just above the distant shore line.

FIR TREE

As you create the fir trees think of the shape you are going to form. Tap up and down lightly using a 1/2 inch angular that you have tapped hard on the palette as you picked up color. I hope you will be able to watch this on P.B.S. to see how hard I hit the palette as I pick up pigment. It opens the brush up. A bristle fan also works but doesn't give as much control, so working them both is great. Change the angle of the brush as you tap lightly. It's far easier to build slowly and not smash in color you cannot get out. Put on some soft mood music, it's always a pleasant background for relaxing and painting.

Apply a mixture of Indigo, Hookers Green Deep and a hint of Ultramarine Blue. Keep your test paper handy to check values. If the color becomes too deep, blot the surface lightly with a soft paper towel. You can always come back and add more pigment. Vary the tree size.

As the tree meets the ground, think about the contour of the land. Rarely would you want to make a straight line at the base. If you tap at an angle follow the contour and pull up a few blades of grass on this uneven line.

With a clean brush, dampen the base of the tree and pull in an irregular pattern to form a shadow on the ground.

EARLY WINTER MORNING continued

ROCKS

The rocks are painted using the 1/2 inch brush with Burnt Sienna and Indigo. Don't over blend the pigment on your palette but allow the colors to mingle on your surface. Think of variety of shape and size keeping the contours of the land in mind as you come down to the snow area. You can again deepen the values as you work. Blotting the surface lightly with a sponge will add a nice texture. Dab with the brush and scrape a little with the handle. Once rocks are applied, with a clean brush, pull a little color from the bottom edge. You may want to add diluted Ultramarine Blue and Violet to the shadow side. See if you should create some reflections in the water area.

DECIDUOUS TREES

Since this is a winter scene the leaves have fallen off the trees and only the trunks and branches are in view. Think about interesting tree shapes. Before you start practice on test paper. The more pressure you apply to the liner, the wider the stroke will appear. Don't make these like telephone poles but instead make graceful lines.

If you balance on your little finger on the surface it is easier to control the liner brush. Make sure your pigment has ink like consistency. Use a liner with a mixture of diluted Indigo and a hint of Burnt Umber. Don't get the trunk lines too dark or they will appear harsh.

While the brush is wet, paint a couple of birds in the distance. Use a liner making them vary in size. Practice on scrap paper to get a feel for the shape you want to make.

FINISHING DETAILS

It's always fun to come back and add finishing details to your painting. Using a liner come back and add a few more grass blades and twigs. Check to see if your trees are reflecting in the water.

Should you want to paint snow back over some of the tree branches, you can break these areas up using Opaque White.

Texture Medium is a really different option and will not only give a snow appearance but will build texture on the rocks and tree branches. Be careful to place in a safe place to dry, you can speed up drying with a hair drier. The painting will shrink some as it dries so don't be afraid to pile it on. Try a greeting card first to learn and practice how this works.

Mats finish a painting. Sometimes you won't want to mat the entire painting but instead find by using a smaller mat or maybe a oval you'll have better composition.

Lightly tap up and down using the angular shader to create the foliage on the fir tree.

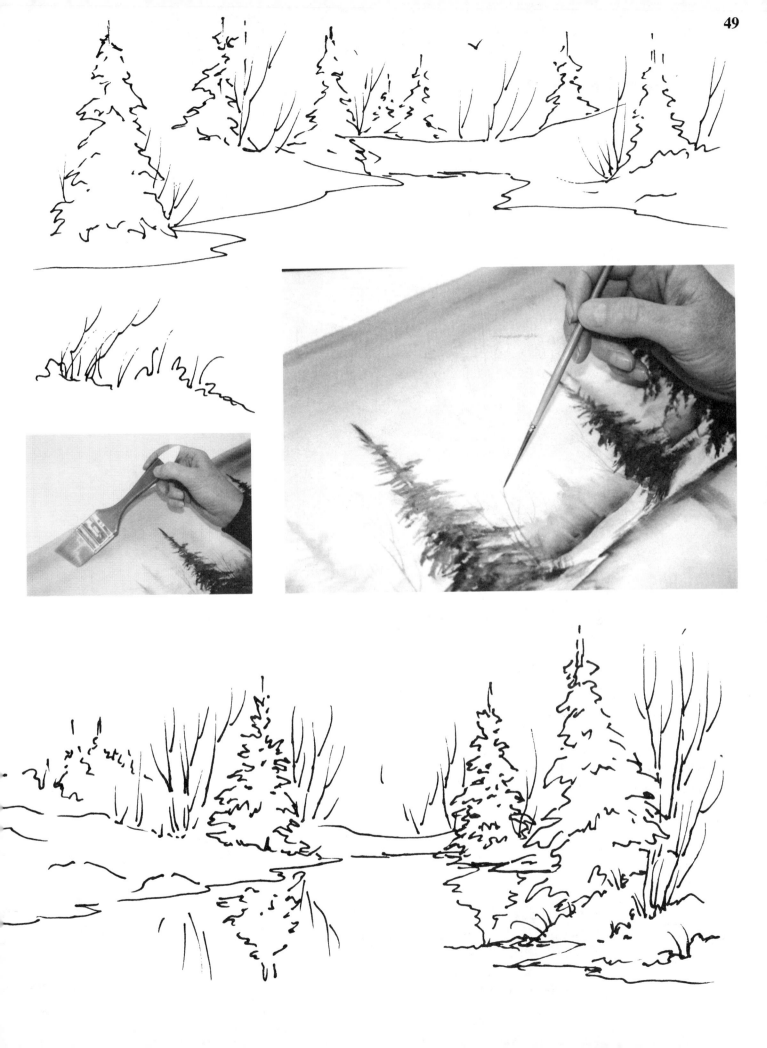

WINTER TOUCH

SUSAN SCHEEWE WATERCOLOR
Ultramarine Blue
Indigo
Turquoise Deep
Burnt Sienna
Country Brick
Hooker Green

SUPPLIES
Sponge
Test Paper
Spray Bottle

BRUSHES
Series S8028, 1-1/2 Inch Background Brush
Series S8010 1/2 Inch Angular Shader
Series S8036   1/2 Inch Foliage Angular
Series S8017 Size 1 Liner

*Texture Medium is a fun application
of texture added to the surface to
create dimension.*

*You could add a few touches on
the foreground branches,
trees and twigs.*

WINTER TOUCH

Before you start to paint or read the instructions, make sure your palette is ready for painting. Spray the palette with clean water to dampen the colors.

In preparation for filming the television series, I will practice a painting many times to figure out what I need to paint and how fast to complete it in 30 or less minutes. While I practice each design I come up with many variations and often it becomes difficult to pick a favorite. So I suggest practicing these on small greeting cards and experiment with color.

Transfer the painting guide onto the watercolor paper with either Saral graphite transferring paper, or do a sketch using a soft pencil. Be careful not to press too hard when transferring the pattern as it is easy to dent the paper. If you dent the paper, color will flow into the recess and it will create a darker appearance.

SKY

Pre-wet the entire sky area with a 1-1/2 inch background angular, paint down to the ground line going around the building area. It's important to apply the pigment while the paper still has a shine. The wet surface will allow the pigment to diffuse easily. Pick up a mixture of Ultramarine Blue and hint of Indigo, adding a touch of Turquoise Deep is optional. Start at the top of the paper making long horizontal strokes. Paint the sky darker towards the top and lighten by adding more water as you work towards the horizon. Try this on a greeting card to test your colors. You may need to re-dampen the surface in the sky area as you work.

DISTANT TREES

It's important to paint these while the sky area is still wet so they will soften and diffuse into the background creating atmosphere and a foggy appearance. Lightly tap the 1/2 inch angular brush up and down, changing direction as you tap to form the tree shapes. Think about variety in size, shape and spacing as you apply the pigment. As the paper starts to dry slightly, tap on a few hints of a deeper value and a hint of Hookers Green could be added as an option. Be careful not to fill the area in solid as you tap on the branches as the pigment will spread or bleed out a bit when it touches the wet pigment.

Don't be afraid to paint some of these trees near the building.

BARN

There is snow on the roof. Be careful not to get this area wet. You can either just be careful or you could protect it with tape or friskit. Use the 1/2 inch angular shader and wet the sides of the building with clean water. Pick up Indigo and Burnt Sienna and apply pigment just under the roof line, rinse the brush and wipe off excess water.

The point of the brush should just be touching the roof line and the short end should be pointed towards the ground. Pull the pigment downward to create the appearance of boards. I prefer using the chisel edge of the angular brush but you might find it more comfortable to use a round brush. A liner could also be used to create the boards.

Should you want more color in your barn, apply a glaze of Country Brick. Windows can be a fun option. You may want to lightly sketch in a window shape with a pencil. Apply a deeper color in the window pane.

It is far easier to use just a little paint. Should a color appear too dark wipe these areas with a clean damp brush.

WATER

Because water is usually transparent it either reflects color from its surroundings or from beneath its surface.

Pre-wet the water area using the angular shader. Pull the brush back and forth in a horizontal direction not a vertical direction when creating the banks edge. While the paper is still shinny apply Ultramarine Blue, Indigo and hint of Turquoise. If you added Hookers Green as a option in the trees carry the color into the water. Add pigment slowly along the edge, pulling down gently. The color will diffuse beautifully. It is far easier to paint water using watercolors than any other medium, so don't be afraid.

FOREGROUND FIR TREES

As you paint the fir tree think about the shape. Practice on a scrap of paper. Use the 1/2 inch angular brush and tap hard on the palette as you pick up mostly Indigo and a hint of Hookers Green that has been diluted. Think about leaving some space for snow and be careful to not make a solid cone shape. Start tapping very lightly on the lower branches. Change the direction as you tap the brush to form a more realistic appearance. You can come back and tap more pigment on to create additional layers and depth.

The base of the tree should follow the terrain. By tapping longer branches on the lower left in a slanted direction, it will create contour against the ground area. Be careful, you don't have your brush too wet or the color will blob out as you tap the surface.

GRASS

There are little blades of grass popping out of the snow. Think about the contour line of the ground as you paint the grassy spots. Tap the brush on the palette to pick up paint, test it on a scrap of paper and practice placing the 1/2 inch angular brush against the surface and then with a sweeping, slightly curled motion lift up. If you pull the brush straight up, the grass will appear stiff and unnatural. You can always add a few blades with the liner. Use the tree colors.

TWIGS AND BRANCHES

Try to make your twigs and branches interesting. Try not to make them too straight like telephone poles with stiff arms. Use a liner with diluted variations of Indigo and hint of Burnt Sienna. You can always go back and make the trunks larger. Try to create a variety in shapes and sizes, it will give it a more realistic appearance. Get a scrap of paper and check the color and the amount of pressure required to form the branches and twigs.

SHADOWS

It's easy to create shadows at the base of the large fir tree and grass areas. Simply wet the surface with clean water under the tree or grass areas. Pull just a little pigment from the tree and grass, be sure to pull the brush when you catch the pigment in a direction that will suggest the contour of the land. This will create a consistency in color, and is a valuable technique in watercolor.

VARIATIONS

There are many variations to this design, you could add a mail box, fence line, or more fir trees. Decorate the mail box with a red ribbon and tap on a green wreath to hang on the barn. A couple of birds in the sky applied with a liner are a great added touch.

You could flip on some snow using Opaque White or White acrylic paint.

I'd love to receive one of the cards you've painted. Happy Painting.

For a great warm up, paint a
greeting card using a small section
including the bird and branches.
It is a wonderful way to test this
technique of plastic wrap.

Experiment with different pigment
strengths creating wonderful variations.

THE FROSTED WINDOW PANE

THE FROSTED WINDOW PANE

SUSAN SCHEEWE WATERCOLORS

Ultramarine Blue
Turquoise Deep
Violet
Indigo
Burnt Sienna
Burnt Umber
Cadmium Yellow Medium
Hunter Green
Hookers Green

BRUSHES

Series S8028 1-1/2 Inch Background Angular
Series S8010 1/2 Inch Angular Shader
Series S8004 Nos. 3 or 5 Round
Series S8001 Liner

MISCELLANEOUS SUPPLIES

Drafting Tape 1/2 Inch Wide
Plastic Wrap - Several Large Pieces
140 or 300 Lb. Cold Pressed.

This is one of my favorite paintings. We have a pine tree outside my kitchen window where little birds hide from the winter winds. I toss bread and seeds out to encourage their return all winter long. In the winters when I was young I loved to see the beautiful designs frost created on the window.

Transfer the painting guide onto the painting surface. It will be helpful draw in a little detail as you transfer the small bird. You may want to transfer the branch lines but it is not necessary to transfer the pine needles.

Using 1/2 inch drafting tape, cover the window frame. You'll see this in the photo for reference. Press the edges of the tape with medium pressure. *It's important the tape is not old or has not sat in the sun or heat because it will become too sticky. The sticky tape would tear the surface when removed. If you are sure about the tape, practice on the edge of a sheet and give a test before you apply it to the entire sheet. A few papers are softer than others and this also could cause the tape to lift the paper.

Once the tape has been applied to the surface don't set it in an area where the sun could heat the surface for a long period. Don't use a hair dryer on the surface while the tape is on as it could heat the backing, making it stick to the surface. It really is fun just following a few guidelines

If you are just starting to paint today it's a good idea to spray the palette with water to dampen the pigments. Spray your palette lightly when your paints start to dry as you continue to paint.

This painting is shown on the P.B.S. series "Scheewe Art Workshop Series One. Call your P.B.S. station for schedule of viewing.

WINDOW PANES

It is important that you pre-wet the area of the window pane but not the snow at the lower section of each frame. Pre-wet these sections using a 1-1/2 inch angular background brush. You will want to apply pigment to these areas while the surface is wet enough to shine. Apply variations of hues using Indigo, Ultramarine Blue and Turquoise Deep keeping in mind watercolors dry lighter. Start with the top three frames. While the window area is wat, lay slightly wrinkled plastic wrap over the top of the paint. Repeat this on the next three frames. When you do the frame area just above the bird be very careful not to pre-wet the bird as well as the snow. Be extra careful as you pre-wet, especially the area around the beak. Again apply the variations of pigment and plastic wrap. *It's important you leave the plastic on the surface to form the beautiful design until the surface becomes dry.* If you lift the plastic while the paper or surface is still very wet the pigment will have a softer edge and not appear as defined. Should the color not appear as dark as you would like you can re-wet the area with clean water, apply more pigment, apply plastic and wait again. Remove plastic but not the tape and you'll be really ready for the next step.

DAY AT THE BEACH
PAGES 104-107

THE FROSTED
WINDOW PANE
PAGES 54-63

WINDOW SNOW

Using a 1/2 inch angular shader, dampen the brush in clean water and remove excess water on a paper towel. Pick up a hint of color variations on the point of the brush, work on the palette for a minute to get a gradation from pigment to only water. Apply the point of the brush towards the bottom window frames applying a little more color towards the corners using variations of Indigo, Ultramarine Blue and hints of Violet. Be careful to allow some of the white paper to remain along the top edge. Don't remove the tape yet.

WALL AREA

It is easier to paint the lower wall area before you remove the tape. Use variation of mixtures of Indigo, and Hunter Green. Making the values deeper just under the window sill. Make uneven vertical strokes, look at the photo for additional reference. Be careful to leave areas to paint the snow and branches.

PULLING TAPE

It is very important that you GENTLY pull off the tape. Should you pull the tape fast you chance tearing the paper. Should the paper start to tear pull the tape from the other side.

BIRD

The eye is small on this little bird. A very common mistake is trying to paint human eyes on animals. Before you start, try to remember to leave a very tiny round area in the upper right *unpainted* to create the highlight. Use the # 3 or # 5 round, removing most of the water and picking up Indigo paint using very little pressure the round eyeball. Should you accidently have lost the white highlight tap it with a dot of Opaque White.

Next leaving an unpainted area next to the eyeball, paint a little Indigo line under the eye and around the top of the eye with Indigo.

Paint the top section of the head with Indigo, still using the round brush with very little pressure. Continue by painting the little dark patch on the chest using Indigo.

Let these areas dry before you do the beak as the color could bleed.

With a clean damp brush soften the color slightly under the eye and along the bottom of the chin line.

Next pick up a little Indigo and Burnt Umber and paint the tail portion. A little variation in color makes it more eye appealing. Wipe a little pigment back off if it becomes solid in appearance.

Paint the top of the wing with variations of Indigo and Burnt Umber. Very lightly work the brush to form the contour. Dilute the pigment leaving a few areas White. Keep in mind the direction of the feathers. Dip the brush back into the mixture and come along the edge of the long feathers on the wing. Tap and pull into the area to create a shadow along the feather transition.

Dampen the lower body area with clean water. Very lightly dab up and down with variations of diluted Indigo and Burnt Umber to create lower body contour, shadow and soft feather appearance.

The beak is next. Using a round brush paint the entire area with diluted Cadmium Yellow Medium. While the area is wet, pick up a hint of diluted Indigo and shade the lower section of the beak and at the top of the beak near the dark section. Wipe immediately if the dark area overtakes the yellow. Watch out that this area doesn't grow too large. The beak line does come back into the head area, refer to photo of the finished painting.

THE FROSTED WINDOW PANE

WINDOW FRAME

The window frames have been painted with a lightly dry brush. Use the 1/2 inch angular shader. Use variations of mixtures of Indigo and Hunters Green. Pick up more of a deep value toward the point of the brush. Set the point of the brush towards the bottom left corner and the shorter end towards the right (there should remain an area on the far right the brush doesn't reach). Sweep the brush towards the top of the paper with a lifting motion. Reload the brush each time you paint an upright frame. Use the same colors as you form the lower area of each frame with a semi dry brush. Leave the top of the horizontal pieces unpainted.

SHADOW UNDER THE BIRD

The shadow area under the bird should be darkest next to the body. Use the 1/2 inch angular and dip the point of the brush in both some Ultramarine Blue, hint of Violet and hint of Indigo. Apply this variation of mixture.

BRANCHES

This would be a great time to be a little nervous and make your hand shake. Painting branches that are too straight can have an unrealistic appearance. Use the round brush with a mixture of Burnt Umber and Burnt Sienna. Be sure to vary the shape and direction you apply pigment.

NEEDLES

Paint the needles with a slight curve. Make a soupy mixture of Hookers Green and Hunter Green. Dip a liner in the pigment, place the point of the brush next to the branch and sweep lifting the brush away from the paper to form a slight taper. Be careful to make lots of needles with a variety of directions including some that cross over each other.

BRANCH SNOW

Come back and paint some shadow on the snow on the branches. Allow some of the paper to remain unpainted. Use the same variation used under the bird.

FINISHING DETAIL

You can always go back and add little finishing touches. You might want to paint a very fine line in the middle of the beak area. You may want to define a few feathers. Let the painting completely dry and step back to see if any more adjustments need to be made. If you are blotting off color don't push the pigment into the surface, instead lightly lift with a light blotting motion.

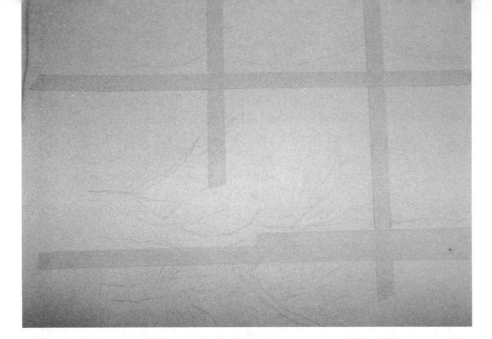

Tape the window frame using 1/2" drafting tape. Be sure to use drafting tape so it will peel off the paper without ripping.

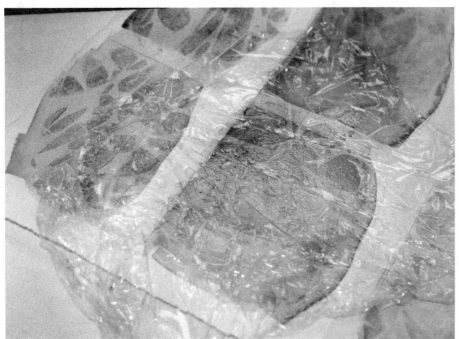

After applying pigment, lay on the plastic wrap. Be sure to allow the paint to dry thoroughly before lifting off the plastic wrap. This insures clean sharp designs in the window.

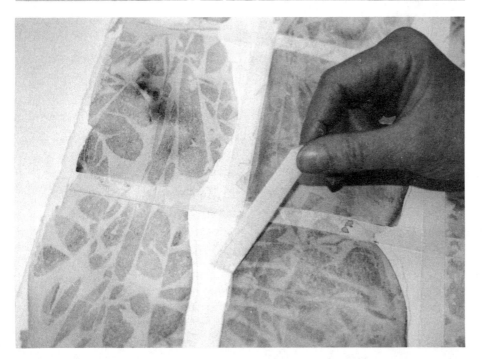

Be sure the paper is completely dry before you start to remove the tape. *GENTLY* pull the tape as you don't want to tear or damage the surface.

MOUNTAIN SPLENDOR

SUSAN SCHEEWE WATERCOLORS
Cobalt Blue
Turquoise Deep
Hunter Green
Hookers Green Deep
Spring Green
Burnt Umber
Burnt Sienna
Country Brick
Opaque White
Cadmium Yellow Pale
Cadmium Yellow Medium
Raw Sienna
Indigo
Violet
Deep Magenta

MARTIN/F WEBER BRUSHES
Series S8004, Size 5 Round
Series S8028, Size 1-1/2 Inch Background
Series S8012, Size 3/4 or 1 Inch Angular Shader
Series S8017, Size 1 Liner
Series S8010, Size 1/2 Angular Shader
Series S8037, Size 3/4 Foliage Brush

Blue Masking Fluid
140 or 300 lb. paper
Soap
Spray Bottle
Tape

We live in an area with beautiful snow capped mountains. They are truly an inspiration for the painting *BUT* if you live in an area with no mountains, simply don't paint them in.

When painting the appearance of a bright sunny day, the colors should have contrast between light and shadows. Shadows play an important role in conveying an impression of bright sunlight.

Transfer or sketch on your painting guide. Make a couple of greeting cards to test color. Before painting, read the forward section on Blue Masking Fluid, which is a masking fluid.

Be sure you remember to first apply soap to your brush before you place it in the Blue Masking Fluid. Rinse your brush every so often and apply soap again before you continue on. Use a round brush to apply the Blue Masking Fluid to form tree trunks, fence, branches and dab on the flowers. Look at the photo for additional help in placement. After this step, you will need to wait for these to dry completely, 20 minutes to an hour depending on humidity. Be sure not to use heat or a hair dryer to speed the drying time because this could cause the Blue Masking Fluid to stick onto the paper and tear it when you remove it.. Since there is such a variety of papers, test the Blue Masking Fluid on a scrap of the paper you plan to use. It always feels rubber like, even when dry. Adjust the sizes of the brushes for smaller paintings.

Don't paint on a flat surface. The portable art studiodrawing board is at a perfect height to comfortably with.

SKY

Pre-wet the entire area down to the mountain tops. Make sure you can see a shine on the surface. While the surface has a shine, apply Cobalt Blue starting at the top of the paper, brushing in long horizontal strokes. Add water to your brush to dilute and lighten the mixture as you work towards the top of the mountains. Adding a hint of lavender or Turquoise Deep are nice variations. The pre-wet surface and the tilt of the drawing board will both make this gradation of color easy to achieve. Don't get deep values behind the tree area, leave it lighter.

MOUNTAIN

Use the 3/4 inch angular shader to paint the mountains. Start on the left side. As you apply pigment, remember the Blue Block will be removed later and there will be clean white paper in those areas. The left side is initially established by wet into wet washes. Start with a diluted mixture of Violet, a hint of Cobalt Blue and Magenta Deep. Come back and deepen the values along the ridges with Violet and Cobalt Blue.

The right side of the mountain is the sunny side. Be careful not to get too much color on them. Apply very diluted tints of mixtures of a little more Cobalt Blue and Violet as you form your ridges.

Concentrate the color variations on the shadow areas and keep the color very light in the sunshine areas. Think about making interesting shapes with the shadows.

There are faint distant mountains behind the trees. Don't get a lot of color in these areas as it could be difficult to cover them when you paint the trees.

DISTANT FIR TREES

Distance creates a decrease in detail. Before you start to create the tree line, think about painting variations in height as they would grow up ridges. Make a mixture of diluted Cobalt Blue with a hint of Indigo and Violet. Swipe the brush using a straight up lifting motion, varying the heights. If you don't pull straight up it will appear as grass rather than distant fir trees. As you go, make an uneven bottom line that you quickly add clean water to soften and lighten the line which makes it easier to create the middleground trees.

MIDDLEGROUND TREES

As you look at the trees in the middleground, you see shapes rather than each leaf being defined. You will want to establish clumps of trees.

Practice with your foliage brush on test paper to find a comfort zone of how it works. Wet into wet with a light tap on an almost dry brush still create a wonderful diffused appearance. If the brush is too wet, the color will just blob out. Tap in a variety of colors, don't mix the color on your palette. Deepen the values at the ground line. Placing the brush in the water container before you start will help the bristle brush to absorb the water and start to fluff out. Use Hookers Green, Hunters Green and a little Spring Green. Don't be afraid to tap down hard on the brush. Vary the height and shape as you tap on. A few touches of yellow are nice as this is a spring scene. Start light and slowly add deeper colors. As the paper starts to dry a little, you'll get a little more leaf definition. When you tap the brush ,pick up a little of your greens and a hint of Indigo to deepen the values. Next, move immediately and quickly into forming the meadow. To form the beginning of the meadow, move and pick up the wet color at the base of the trees. If you wait until the tree area dries it could be difficult to move the paint.

MEADOW

With a clean brush, catch the color at the base of the trees. Wet the entire field area and then near the bottom pick up a little Spring Green. Then near the path apply a little Cobalt Blue and a hint of Indigo with a touch of varied greens. Tap the brush up and down to give the feeling of distant grass.

FOREGROUND TREE FOLIAGE

Lightly start tapping on tree foliage. You'll continue to build these areas so allow the sky to shine through the foliage. Think about uneven patterns, don't just tap up and down once because it will not look natural. Instead tap up and down in an uneven fashion. Use variations of Hookers Green, Hunters Green and a little Spring Green. You'll be coming back to this area so don't overwork it.

PATH

Pre-wet the path area. Pre-wet a larger path than you plan to see in the finished painting. Use the angular brush and pick up yellow first (diluted Cadmium Yellow Pale and Cadmium Yellow Medium) and apply down the path with a curving motion to create contour. Next pick up a little diluted Raw Sienna and apply towards the bottom of the path. Next pick up a hint of Country Brick and apply at the lower section working for a gradation in color. Next deepen the color to create shadows along the edges, using Burnt Umber and Burnt Sienna continue to form the contour. Be careful not to lose the light area.

FOREGROUND FLOWERS

Before you apply the greens, start with the foreground flowers. Use the foliage brush to tap on brilliant flowers. While I used Cobalt Blue, hints of Violet or Magenta Deep can be a beautiful variation. You can always tone these areas down with green later, but you'll never get pretty bright flower colors if you put the green on first. It's time to spray your palette with clean water to refresh the color.

FOREGROUND FOLIAGE

Use the foliage brush to create the appearance of both bushes and grass. Start by tapping on variations of green with a few hints of Indigo varying the values. Leave some areas unpainted at first so you can come back later and tap on lighter greens using Spring Green and Indigo. Sweep the foliage brush upward, curving to create grass. Get that test paper to test this technique first. Time to take a breath. Use a liner and pull up some detailed grass blades.

REMOVING BLUE MASKING FLUID

Use a piece of masking tape or watercolor tape to remove the Blue Masking Fluid. Use the tape as you would use it if you were taking lint off your clothes. Be gentle as you remove the Blue Masking Fluid. Make sure the paper is dry before you start to remove.

TREE TRUNKS AND FENCE POST

In sunshine the light strikes trees and fence posts with bright more vivid yellows. Apply these spots of sunshine with the 5 round, using diluted Cadmium Yellow Pale and Raw Sienna. Apply shadows with Burnt Umber and Burnt Sienna on the shadow areas and the left side. Create a random pattern.

TREE FOLIAGE

Tap foliage brush back over the tree trunks and branches lightly. Create a beautiful and graceful pattern with a delicate tap.

WHITE FLOWERS

You may want to come back and tap on a few dots of Raw Sienna and Cadmium Yellow Medium in a few of the white flowers. Don't paint a center in every white area. Pull a hint of background color into a few of the white areas to give a tint of color.

BUSHES

Use a liner with a diluted mixture of Burnt Umber and Burnt Sienna to create graceful lines on the twigs and trunk lines. Tap back over these with a little of your greens using your foliage brush.

FENCE WIRE

With a liner and diluted Burnt Umber paint the fence wire. Be careful not to make it too straight. Make a twined appearance to the wire.

FINISHING

Come back with a liner and develop twigs on the branches. Add a few faint lines in the middleground trees. Pull up graceful grass lines. Deepen the values under the clumps of foliage on the trees.

If you have covered the surface with pigment and have not left any clean white highlight areas, use Opaque White and put the highlights in. If this doesn't work, you can add a mixture of Opaque White and color for the highlights. Be very careful not to use too much Opaque White as it will create the loss of the delicate transparent watercolors.

Be sure to soap the brush when applying Blue Masking Fluid.

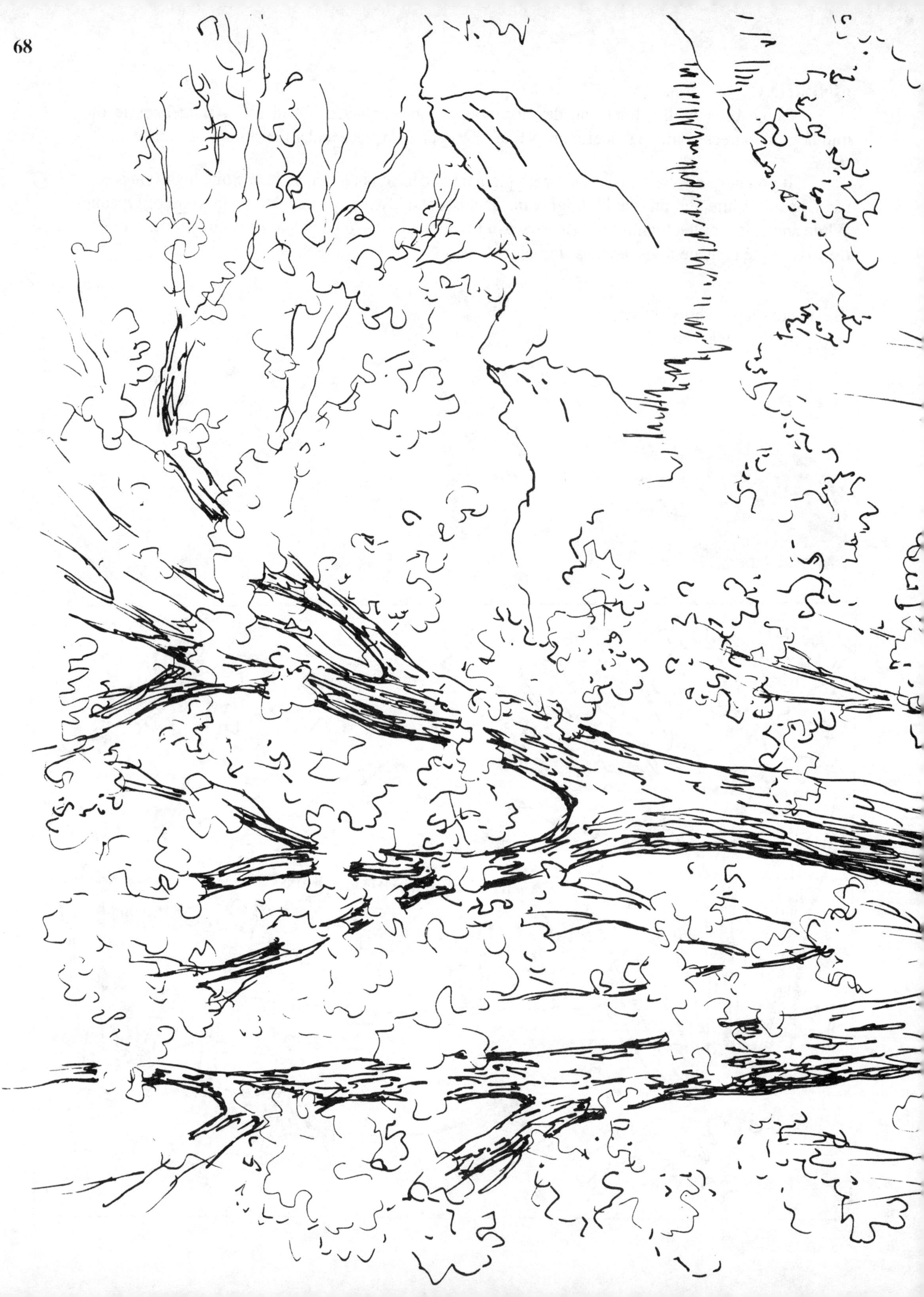

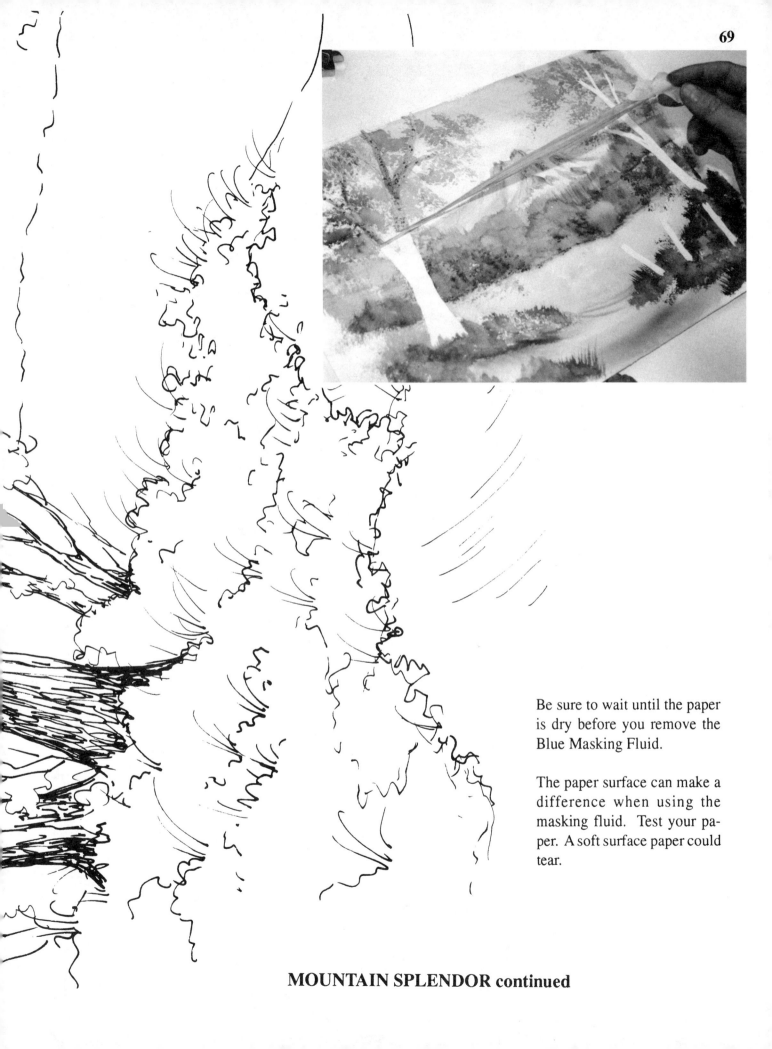

Be sure to wait until the paper is dry before you remove the Blue Masking Fluid.

The paper surface can make a difference when using the masking fluid. Test your paper. A soft surface paper could tear.

MOUNTAIN SPLENDOR continued

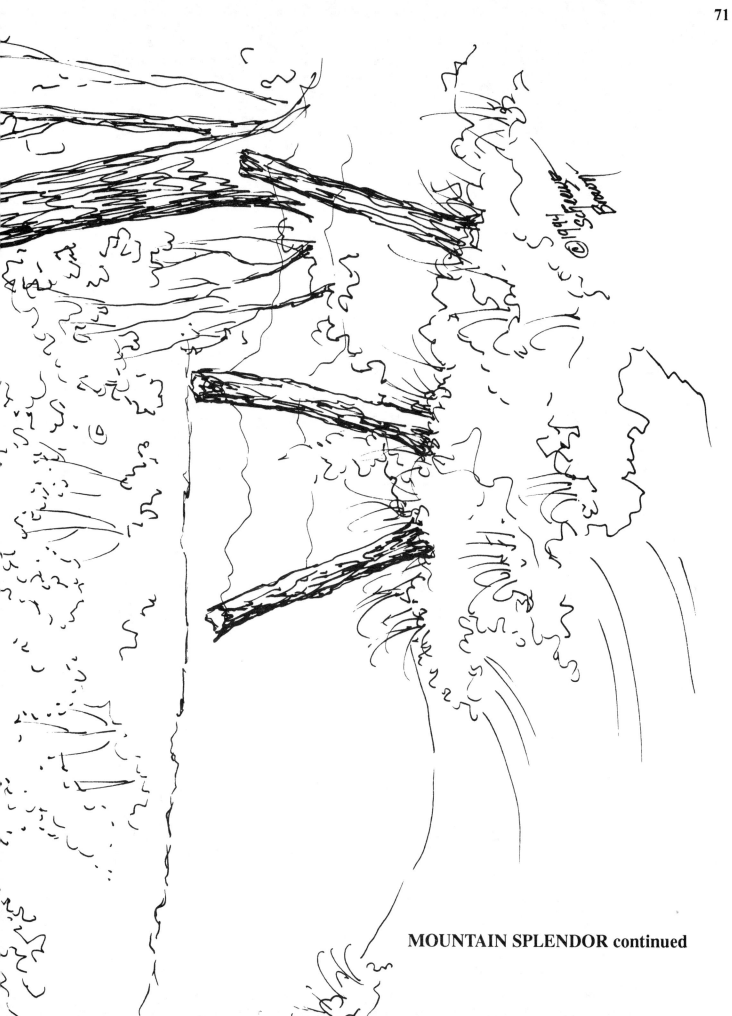

MOUNTAIN SPLENDOR continued

TOUCHES OF BLUE

©1994
Scheewe
Brown

There are several ways to create the appearance of a scalloped edge. The photo shows the use of a tape that can be used to easily create the edge. This tape is very effective on the edge of a greeting card, but you could paint on the scalloped appearance with out the tape or you could use Blue Masking Fluid to form the shapes you desire.

Be sure you wait until the surface is dry before removing the tape or masking fluid.

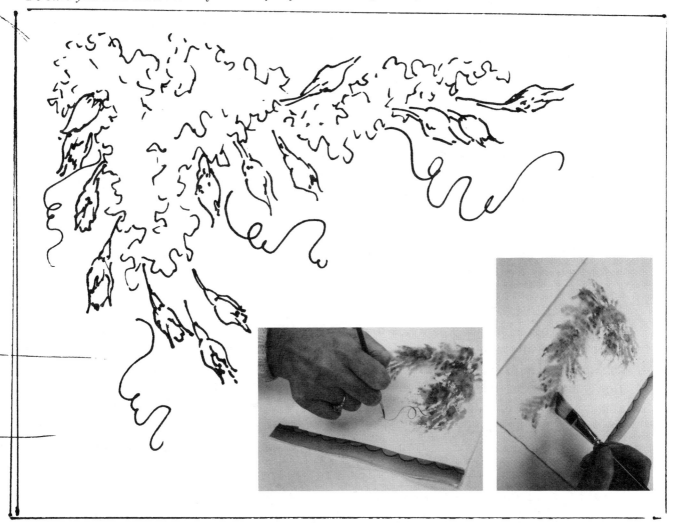

TOUCHES OF BLUE

SUSAN SCHEEWE WATERCOLOR

Brilliant Cranberry
Magenta Deep
Violet
Hunters Green
Hookers Green
Indigo
Ultramarine Blue
Cobalt Blue

BRUSHES

Series S8012 3/4 Inch Foliage Brush
Series S8001 No. 1 Liner
Series S8010 1/2 Inch Angular Shader

Stencil Tape
Stencil
140 lb. Cold Pressed Paper

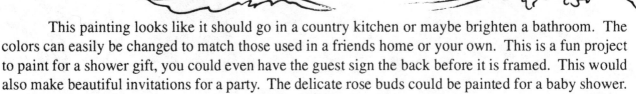

This painting looks like it should go in a country kitchen or maybe brighten a bathroom. The colors can easily be changed to match those used in a friends home or your own. This is a fun project to paint for a shower gift, you could even have the guest sign the back before it is framed. This would also make beautiful invitations for a party. The delicate rose buds could be painted for a baby shower.

You might leave space at the bottom to write a special recipe or message. Experiment, have a lot of greeting cards handy, and play around with the many color variations.

Using stencils can be lots of fun when creating a painting. I hope you'll experiment with the many ways that this technique can be applied to your watercolors. I used tape designed to create a pattern for this painting. The tape comes in a variety of patterns, plus there are a number of commercially made stencils that also could be used.

This is a very simple flower container. You may wish to make a sketch of a container of your choice or transfer the painting guide.

The tape I used comes on a strip with three parts. Apply the strip to the top of the container as this will form both the rim and pattern. Pull back the center section after you have laid down the strip. Refer to the photo as a reference. You'll put pigment in this area to create a border design.

SCALLOPED AREA

You'll find it easier if you pre-wet the paper, which will aid in achieving a consistent color gradation. Use the 1/2 inch angular brush to pre-wet the scalloped section. Use either Ultramarine Blue, Cobalt Blue or a mixture of both to paint the area. Pick up more pigment on the point of the brush and deepen the area on each edge. Wipe off a little pigment in the center area with a clean damp brush or sponge if necessary to create a nice gradation of color. Don't speed up drying time with a hair dryer, the head will make the tape become sticky and tear the surface when removed. Let this dry completely before you remove the tape.

BACHELOR BUTTONS

The bachelor buttons are easy to paint. They come in so many beautiful shades of blues and lavenders you may want to try several variations. Using the 1/2 inch angular shader, pick up Ultramarine pigment on the point of the brush, place the point of the brush towards the outside edge of the flower and the short side near the center, pull the brush back and forth to create the ragged edge. The center of the flower should appear lighter at this stage. You could either lift a little color out of the center or add a little deeper value to the edge. A hint of Violet or Magenta Deep are both great variations. If you have created your own sketch be sure to paint a few buds beside the full flowers. You come back to these later.

ROSE BUDS

The rose buds are painted next. I've used a beautiful new color called Brilliant Cranberry. The bud shape is wider at the base than at the top. Start by picking up more pigment on the point of the brush creating a gradation of color along the chiseled edge. The deeper values should be along the base and then a few little deep taps of pigment at the top of the rose bud. You'll need to wait until the paper dries before you paint the green section or it will bleed together.

HEATHER

It's very helpful if you place your foliage brush in water for a few minutes before you paint the foliage, this will spread the bristles apart making it easier to work with. Wipe some of the water off the brush, this is not a dry brush technique, but it is also important that the brush is not to wet. Tap the brush in a little Hunters Green and Hookers Green, then test it on a scrap paper. Too much water will make it bleed together, too little and the Heather pattern will be too fine. Tap up and down changing the pressure and position where you plan to apply pigment. Tap a little over the bachelor buttons but stay away from the rose buds. Give the brush a really good rinse. With a clean brush pick up a variety of mixtures using Violet and Magenta Deep. Tap this on delicately to create the flower pattern of the heather, it can be tapped slightly over the buds. Think about creating a graceful curve the heather stems. You may need to go back and lightly tap on more variations.

CONTAINER

Now you can gently pull off the tape. Surprise, see how the scallops remain crisp as well as the top edge of the container. Using the 1/2 inch angular brush pre-wet the entire container being careful to not wash into the scalloped area. While the surface is still wet, pick up Ultramarine Blue on the point of the brush. Place the point of the brush towards the outside edge to shade the container. It's easy to get a lovely gradation of color. A hint of Violet adds a nice variation. Don't forget to do the top section.

ROSE BUDS

The green area on the rose buds can be painting using either a No. 5 round or a 1/2 inch angular shader. Use a green of your choice, some suggestions are Hookers Green, Hunters Green or even a touch of Turquoise added is nice. Start at the base of the bud making the calyx rounder towards the base, pull the brush and lifting up on the pressure as you move towards the top of the buds.

FILLER BLADES

With the same mixture used on the green area of the bud, paint lots of filler blades. You can use a No. 5 round or a finer brush to make the filler blades. Using very little pressure start by pressing-down near the bouquet and then lift up slowly to form a graceful taper.

TABLE AREA

You will want to pre-wet the table area with a 1-1/2 inch background brush so the pigment will diffuse easily. Be sure to carefully bring a little color up on both sides of the container. I used Cobalt Blue, but you might add a hint of violet or a pattern to the table area.

BACHELOR BUTTON CENTERS

Using either the point of the angular shader or a round brush paint dots in the center of the bachelor buttons. Tap up and down lightly using a mixture of Violet and Ultramarine Blue.

DIMENSIONAL POPPIES

SUSAN SCHEEWE WATERCOLORS

Brilliant Cranberry   Chinese White
Orange   Hookers Green Deep
Cadmium Red Light   Hunters Green
Magenta Deep   Ultramarine Blue
Turquoise Deep   Violet
Indigo

BRUSHES

S8010 1/2 Inch Angular Shader
S8013 1 Inch Angular Shader
S8017 Size 1 Liner

MISCELLANEOUS SUPPLIES

140 lb. or 300 lb. Cold Pressed Paper
Texture Medium
Spray Bottle

Using texture medium will add a new dimension to your painting. Make a similar sketch or transfer the painting guide onto your watercolor paper. Scoop some texture medium on your 1/2 inch angular shader. Roll or twist the brush slightly to remove the medium from the brush onto your surface. The texture medium is designed to create texture and dimension, unlike gesso that would crackle. The medium will shrink slightly as it drys. The drying period depends on the amount of medium applied to the surface and humidity. It's best to apply the texture medium the day before you plan to paint to ensure is thoroughly dry before applying glazes over the top. It is a good idea to do a couple trial runs on greeting cards before doing a larger painting. It is difficult to pick a favorite color of poppy, as they come in so many luscious shades.

POPPIES

Very often I paint poppies with a deeper color in the center, but on this painting I've kept more color toward the outside edge of the petals. Start with the back petals and work forward. Pre-wet each petal prior to applying color, this will give you more working time verses painting on a dry surface. The texture will help greatly to add a dimensional appearance. Apply Brilliant Cranberry on the tip of the 1/2 inch angular shader, place the point of the brush to the edge of the petal with the short end towards the center. Pull the color along the top edge of each petal and then rinse the brush, adding water to lighten the value towards the center. You may want to deepen the value of the ruffle on the back side by adding Magenta Deep. A few touches of Orange and Cadmium Red Light are nice. Be careful not to get color in the very center pod.

Still using red values, paint the next two petals. Apply more pigment along the top edge of each petal and again dilute this with a lot of clean water as you work towards the base.

Turn your paper or board around so you can reach your petals at an easy angle. You'll find it much easier to paint the bottom petals when your hand is in a good writing position. Again, apply deeper color to the outside edge on the petal and dilute with water as you come to the center.

CENTER POD

Start by painting a foundation using a mixture of diluted Hookers Green Deep with a hint of diluted Turquoise Deep. Apply the pigment with the 1/2 inch angular shader, apply more pigment to deepen the hue and value towards the lower section of each pod.

WAIT until the area has completely dried before you apply lines which appear in the center. Use a liner with Indigo to form the line work on top of the pod. Paint an uneven dot pattern using a liner

WATERFALL SPLASH
PAGE 96-103

TOUCHES OF BLUE
PAGES 72-75

with Indigo around the outside of the pod. Be careful not to line these dots up in a row, refer to the photo for additional help with color placement.

BACKGROUND AND LEAVES

Pre-wet the background area using a 3/4 or 1 inch flat brush, be somewhat careful around the shape but don't worry if a little color bleeds out into the background. The paper should be evenly wet, no dry spots or puddles. It is easier to pre-wet one section at a time or about half the background.

The texture medium will help create the leaves, but the first application of color should be faint and it will diffuse softly into the wet background. Once this first application has been painted, come back and add more detail and additional glazes. Use variations of diluted Hunters Green, Hookers Green, Indigo and Turquoise Deep. You can use even hints of Violet and Ultramarine Blue. It is very helpful to have a test paper handy to check values and hues.

Vary the size, shape and color of these leaves. Using the 1/2 inch angular shader come back and add glazes. Apply more pigment toward the point of the brush, place the point of the brush on both sides of the vein leaving the original wash showing through. Should you need to lighten the vein, wipe the brush edge on the vein with a clean angular shader.

Come back with additional glazes to deepen the values on some of the background leaves. Use the photograph for a reference but have fun and make your own variations .

FINISHING

When you step back you may see some adjustments are needed. You can wipe back areas with a damp brush or add more pigment.

If you need to apply more texture medium wait until it has dried completely before you apply pigment. While you can add pigment into the texture medium you'll get a different appearance.

Experiment on the greeting cards. I would truly enjoy receiving a card from you that you painted, and to here how your coming along. It is fun to see the many beautiful variations that can be painted.

82

DIMENSIONAL POPPIES

*Make sure the texture medium
is dry before you start to paint.*

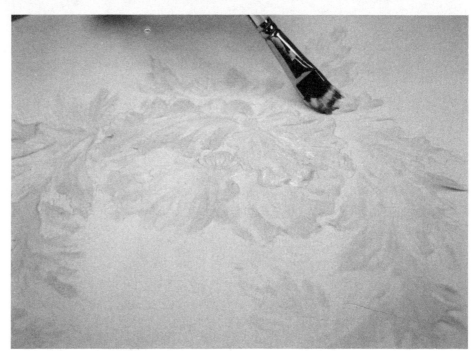

The creamy consistency of Texture Medium makes it easy to create wonderful texture with a brush. Modeling paste is stiffer, not as easy to use and works best with a painting knife.

GARDEN GATE

The foliage brush makes creating the garden in bloom very easy.

© 1994
Scheewe
Braun

GARDEN GATE

"GARDEN GATE"

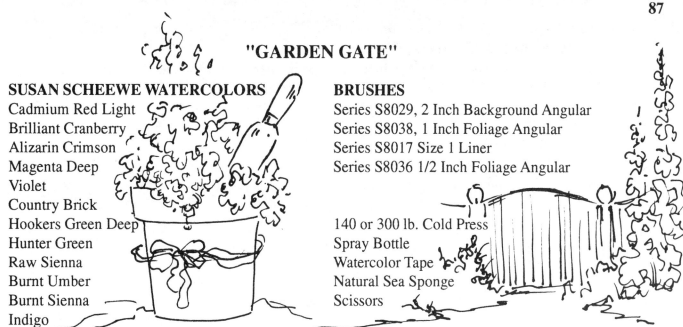

SUSAN SCHEEWE WATERCOLORS
Cadmium Red Light
Brilliant Cranberry
Alizarin Crimson
Magenta Deep
Violet
Country Brick
Hookers Green Deep
Hunter Green
Raw Sienna
Burnt Umber
Burnt Sienna
Indigo

BRUSHES
Series S8029, 2 Inch Background Angular
Series S8038, 1 Inch Foliage Angular
Series S8017 Size 1 Liner
Series S8036 1/2 Inch Foliage Angular

140 or 300 lb. Cold Press
Spray Bottle
Watercolor Tape
Natural Sea Sponge
Scissors

This is one of my very favorite paintings. It can easily be adjusted in size and while making fantastic greeting cards it looks equally beautiful done as a large painting. The flowers can easily be adjusted to colors of your choice. It was truly difficult to pick a favorite as I did some in blues and some in pinks and lavenders. The mats can change the appearance of the finished painting again depending on how far you extend both the flower garden and the path.

There was a garden gate much like this we saw when we were taking a drive. The bright sunshine hit on the dazzling flowers and the yard beyond the gate was in the shadows from tall trees. Make changes in the gate if you have one similar in mind. Enjoy the beautiful splash of color.

Transfer the painting guide or make a sketch with a graphite pencil. Take the watercolor tape or drafting tape and secure it to the surface. Tape comes in a variety of widths, it is handy to have a couple of widths available for your paintings. Cut pieces to shape the fence line you desire. You could use a friskit in this area if you live in a rural area and finding drafting tape to purchase is difficult. Depending on your paper, test the corner of the paper to see if the tape sticks. Don't use old tape that has become too sticky. Most masking tape is too sticky but will work on a watercolor paper with a harder surface.

PREPARATION

You may want to stretch the paper if you plan on doing a large painting on 140 lb. cold press. You don't need to stretch 300 lb. cold pressed paper. Pre-wet the paper using a size 2 background angular and brush right down to the horizon line going over the gate. Be sure to get this evenly wet. You will need to work fast as the wet on wet technique requires the dampness of the paper. Read all the instructions before wetting the paper.

Be sure to spray your palette and have lots of paint ready to use. Have a spray bottle with clean water a spray bottle that you've mixed Brilliant Cranberry to a very fluid consistency.

DISTANT YARD

The distant yard is full of a variety of green values. Use variations of mixtures applied with the 2 inch background brush, use Hookers Green, Hunters Green, Indigo and even a few hints of Burnt Umber mixed in. Don't overwork the area and turn it all into a uniform mass. Spray the surface lightly to keep the surface workable. Come back with a damp sea sponge and blot up and down creating a realistic mottled patter. Leave areas open and unpainted to paint the flowers. If you don't leave clean areas the flowers will never be brilliant.

DISTANT YARD (Continued)

Put the 1 inch foliage brush in the water container to soak for a few minutes before you start to paint on flowers. You may want to sponge on a little more color just behind the bottom of the fence.

FENCE LINE

While the background is still wet, use the plastic beveled handle to scratch the surface and create a fence line. The pigment should flow into the scratched area giving a darker value and as it starts to dry you'll lift out pigment. Once the entire area is dry this technique won't work. You can try spraying with clean water to re-wet the area and give it a try or let the paper dry completely and come back with a liner and paint the wire with Indigo and a hint of Opaque White.

FLOWERS

To create the lacy filigree of the flowers, color must be tapped on clean paper to appear bright. Lightly spray the surface of the paper where you plan to tap on flowers. Hold the 1 inch brush upright and tap up and down lightly. The color choice is hard to pick. On the television series I started with painting the flowers Brilliant Cranberry. These flowers are not detailed but are meant to create the impression of flowers. If you wish to put on more detail splash on the flowers and come back and refine these areas later. Take into consideration as you tap on color, the pattern and overall composition. I dilute the colors somewhat on my palette but allow them to mingle and flow together on the paper.

FOLIAGE AND GRASS

It is fun to continue to add greens by tapping with the foliage brush lightly. Don't tap so hard you accidently lose all your bright flower colors. You may want to lightly spray the area with clean water to create a soft diffused effect. Once this area is dry you can come back with a liner or round brush and add details.

At the bottom edge of the green re-wet the edge of the color and let it flow into the path area.

PATH AND STEPS

Make sure the area is wet along the edges as well as in the path area to create a foundation of color. Apply a diluted mixture of Country Brick and Burnt Umber using the angular shader. Start up at the fence line and come down over the path area. Add a little more pigment towards the grass and flower borders.

Come back and add more pigment at the base of the bottom fence cross board. The top of the stair should be light so don't pull down too much color. I love to add a few dabs of lavender and blues. Test paper will make your choice easier. If you paint the path colors on test paper you can lay the test paper on your painting and you can judge if you like it.

FENCE

Be careful as you remove the tape. If you rip at the tape or give it a quick jerk you very likely will damage the paper. If you pull gently you shouldn't have a problem but if you see one starting to tear the surface, pull the tape from the other end.

Don't worry if a little color slipped along the edge, it will add to the character of the fence. You should pick up color as you dampen the fence with clean water off the edges. As you paint the brace boards pull more color from the background or add a hint of diluted Indigo and Violet to create a shadow.

Pull some diluted Violet and Indigo on the fence line but use a damp brush and lightly drop on the surface crating a somewhat grained effect. The variations are unlimited so once again if you think you might want to use other colors put them on a scrap of test paper and then lay them against the surface.

the surface crating a somewhat grained effect. The variations are unlimited so once again if you think you might want to use other colors put them on a scrap of test paper and then lay them against the surface. Be sure you tuck the side section of the fence into the flower bed. Tap some of the flower colors backup over the bottom and side.

STEPS

The steps are painted next. They are not brand new so be careful not to paint the area too straight. They'll appear far more realistic with a slight curvature as though they have been worn over time. Be mindful to use to get a lot of variety in color values, dab them in lightly.

ROCKS

Cover the painting leaving only the path uncovered. You can either splatter diluted paint with a brush or you may mix some diluted paint and apply with a sponge or spray bottle. Having a variety of the colors you've splattered, will once again give a rich realistic look of a country path.

FINISHING

Come back with a liner and a mixture of Burnt Umber and Indigo. Paint a latch on the gate.

Step back and see if you want to apply a few deeper values in your flowers as they may lighten more than you planned as they dried. You can dampen an area with a clean sponge and lift a little paint if you feel an area became too dark.

Try doing several greeting cards with variations while you still are in the mood.

Remember mats can will the appearance of a painting. You can think of a variety of styles that will work wonderfully.

I truly hope this will soon become one of your favorites.

GARDENER'S OLD FREIND
"WATERING CAN"

We have always had pansies growing in our yard. I remember as a little girl my grandma picking them to bring into her home. How fun to paint these flowers with special memories.

Be sure to start with the back petals as you create these flowers.

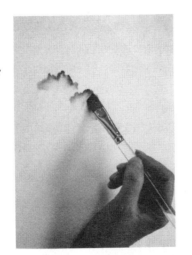

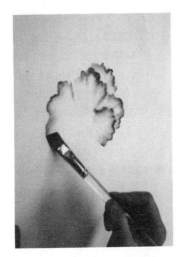

GARDENERS OLD FRIEND "WATERING CAN"

SUSAN SCHEEWE WATERCOLORS
Cadmium Yellow Pale
Cadmium Yellow Medium
Raw Sienna
Spring Green
Hookers Green
Hunter Green
Indigo
Turquoise Deep
Violet
Magenta Deep

SUSAN SCHEEWE BRUSHES
Series 8005 Size 6 Round Brush
Series 8012 3/4 Inch Angular Brush
Series 8010 1/2 Inch Angular Brush
Series 8017 Size 1 Liner

140 lb. or 300 lb. Cold Pressed
Sponge
Spray Bottle

Just a suggestion. It is important to read through the instructions and not jump ahead for you could end up with more problems than success.

The inspiration for this painting came from a watering can I purchased at a country fair with my daughter. It was a fun day and each time I look at this painting it brings back those memories. I so enjoy the charms of aged, old watering cans that I've started a small collection. You may have a favorite watering can of your own that you would like to paint, it is easy to substitute it by making a sketch.

You may want to warm up for the larger painting by experimenting with several small greeting cards. Read the instructions completely before you start and apply much the same technique using smaller brushes. I've added some sketches of the small pansies that could be used on cards. These cards would make treasured shower invitations, one that a bride or mother-to-be would remember for years to come.

Start by transferring the pattern guide to the paper. Be careful to use the proper transfer paper as there are some that resist water. Test your transfer paper first on a separate sheet to ensure you have selected the proper type.

WATERING CAN

When painting the watering can leave the top rim and the areas behind the flowers and leaves unpainted, these will be painted later in the instructions.

The first area to start painting will be the yellow areas on the watering can, it's important to place these in now to assure bright colors. Using a round brush apply Cadmium Yellow Medium on the rim of the spout, top of the neck and at the base of the spout (refer to photo). Come back and add Raw Sienna to shade these areas and add more contour.

Next you'll start painting on the watering can doing separate sections; starting with the spout arm, then the main body, handle at the top of can, side handle, spout and last the rim. Be sure to not paint the rim until last and you need to paint these separately so that the do not blend together. You may find it easier if you pre-wet some of these areas. My charming country water can is a deep green but I selected medium greens for the painting

Paint variations of diluted mixtures of Hookers Green, Hunters Green, Turquoise Deep and hints of Indigo. Use a 1/2 inch angular brush starting by picking up more pigment on the point of the brush. The entire brush will be on the surface of the spout arm with the point of the brush towards the outside edge of the arm. Later in the painting we will paint the spout and rim. Pull along the outside edge of the arm, pull downward on each side and then quickly rinse the brush of paint and wash the paint from the sides to create a gradation in color. Lift out color towards the center by washing a small amount of water over it then picking up color with a dry brush to create a uniform value.

Next reload the angular brush again, pick up more pigment on the point of the brush, place the point of the brush next the yellow band at the base of the neck and around the lower section by the rim, rinse the brush to pull back and lighten the pigment. A touch of Violet is used to create the appearance of a reflection. Don't over blend the colors, the soft variations will create a far more interesting and realistic appearance.

Use a mixture of diluted Hunters Green and Turquoise Deep, base in the main body of the watering can.. Pick up more of these pigments plus add a hint of indigo on the point of the angular shader and deepen the color under the rim and towards the outside edges. Also, paint the shadow area cast from the flowers and leaves. Pull a little color across to create the appearance of ribs in the metal, refer to the photo. Wipe out areas with a clean damp brush should the color become to uniform. The handle at the top can be painted next. Paint the center area on the handle first and allow this to dry before you paint the rim on each edge. Again use the angular shader, apply more pigment at the top and on the shadow created by both rims.

Paint the side handle using either your angle shader or round brush using the same beautiful variations. With a damp angular brush apply a light glaze of Violet over the top of both handles. Use a round brush to paint the spout, apply a very diluted wash of Turquoise and Hunters Green, allow this area to dry. Next paint the spout rim after it has dried thoroughly, then come back and detail the rib sections on the side with deeper values.

You most likely will be able to pull enough color off the edge to paint the rim section With a damp round brush, wipe a little color off the edge to create light color variations. You can always add a hint of color from your palette should this area not get light enough.

PANSIES

Note, not all of the flowers and buds are facing forward, think of how flowers grow in nature and keep this in mind as you paint along.

Pansies come in many beautiful color combinations it is truly hard to pick a favorite, even on the same plant each flower has a unique variation of colors. Each flower has 5 petals, 4 smaller top petals and 1 large lower petal. Each pansy has a little face, the lower large petal often appears to be a mouth, with eyes on the two petals directly above or in the middle of the flower.

Start by placing Cadmium Yellow Pale at the top center of the large lower petal. Place the point of the brush at the very center and pull out some. Come back and while the area is still wet apply a little Cadmium Yellow Medium to shade this area. Paint all of the large forward facing pansies lower petal in the same manner.

While the lower petals are still wet pick up variations of Magenta Deep, Ultramarine Blue and Violet on the point of the angular brush, or use a color of your choice. Place the point of the angular brush on the outside edge of the petal with the short side of the brush facing inward towards the center. Pull across with a little curve and twist motion to create the ruffled edge on the flowers. Should the yellow area start to dry come back with a clean damp brush and wipe over the area so the colors will defuse. While this area is still damp, with a liner or the point of an angular brush lightly paint on the outward sweeping lines of the bottom pansy petal using Violet and Magenta Deep. Continue with the variation of colors, apply the point to the outside edge painting all back two petals on all the forward flowers. When you do the two middle petals apply more Violet and Blue, while the petals are still damp, paint the darker color that wings outward with a liner (refer to photo).

GARDENERS OLD FRIEND
"WATERING CAN"

BUDS

Use the same variations of colors when creating these sections keeping more color towards the outside edge of the petal.

Use a liner to apply green color mixtures at the top of the bud and stem. Start with the stem using a little Hookers Green Deep and Hunters Green. Next to the crown of the stem use a little more pressure on the brush, lifting up on the pressure as you work towards the end of each section. Come back with a few diluted hints of Violet mixed into the greens to pull color together.

LEAVES

The angular shader comes in a variety of sizes while most often I use a 1/2 inch angular shader you might feel more comfortable using a 3/8 or 1 inch angular shader. To diffuse the leaf shapes I use the point of the brush towards the outside edge but the entire brush is on the surface of the paper. Apply variations of diluted Spring Green and Hunters Green. Allow this diluted color to dry a little before you start painting more pigment to create separation and depth.

Pick up medium to deep values of Hunters Green and Hookers Green on the point of the brush, test the brush on a scrap or test paper to check the value and to see if you have a even gradation of color While the entire brush will be on the surface think of the point much as a pointed round brush but with the bonus of blended color. Apply the deeper values on each leaf to create shading where they would fall behind other leaves or flowers. Leave the vein area with the original wash showing through and glide the brush along each side of the vein lifting towards the ends of each leaf. The vein of the leaf is lighter than the rest of the leaf. You may need to go back and lift color out of the vein area with a clean damp cloth.

GROUND AREA

Before you apply pigment to the ground area, pre-wet a very large area using a 3/4 or 1 inch angular shader. Wet a far larger area then you plan to apply pigment to and look for a slight shine.

I've applied a mixture of diluted Burnt Umber and diluted Country Brick with dabs of diluted Magenta Deep and diluted Hunters Green. Slowly dab or pat on more color to deepen the values adding more paint where the shadow would be cast from leaves and the watering can. Pat with a damp sponge or soft towel; a soft sponge will create a lovely texture.

FINISHING

Take a break and walk away from your painting for a few minutes or a day or two. Come back and you can easily see if you need to make a couple adjustments. Check to see if you have added the stems and veins.

You may wish to add a few washes of diluted Violet to create a reflective color.

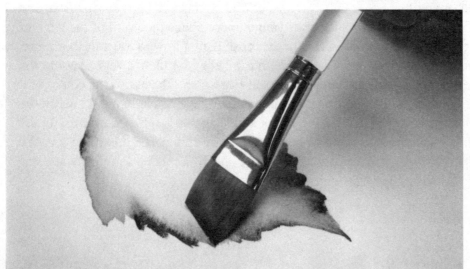

The angular shader makes it easy to create a gradation of colors. Put more pigment on the point of the brush.

The resist stick is extremely helpful in creating the "Watercolor Splash". Practice on a card or scrap paper before you start the painting to get a feel for the results.

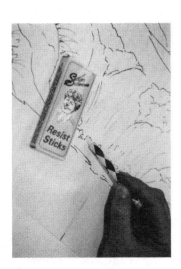

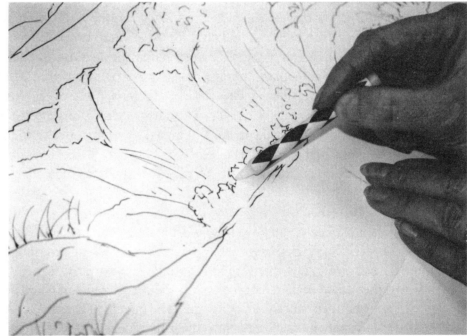

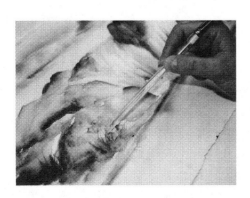

Use the handle of the brush to pull up pigment.

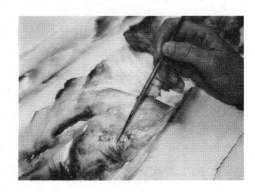

"WATERFALL SPLASH"

You will find it easy to create splash and sparkling jets of water when using the resist stick. One beautiful afternoon we took the scenic drive just 15 minutes from our house in the Columbia Gorge near Multnomah Falls. It has so many beautiful small waterfalls that I was so inspired to come home and paint one of those sparkling falls. You may have some photos of falls you've visited that you'd like to sketch on the paper with a graphite pencil or use the painting guide. This is such a fun painting and easy to make many wonderful variations of. Do a sketch on a couple of greeting cards to give yourself a chance to practice color variations and experiment with how the resist stick works.

When using the resist stick the areas which you apply it to will repel the watercolor pigment. Read the section on the resist stick at the front of the book before doing this painting and test this technique on a scrap of paper before you apply the wax to the painting surface.

Plan the areas where you want to add sparkle in your painting. Make an uneven line at the top of the splash area. Use the stick to create the shape you desire just as you would a brush. The contour is important in creating the shape and form of the shimmering water that splashes down the falls. The direction you pull the stick will be important, along with the pressure.

You might want to apply a few horizontal lines in the lower pond area. (Refer to the photo).

TOP BANK AREA

Start at the top of the paper using a 1-1/2 inch angular background brush to pre-wet the paper, going over the distant bank, rocks and top of the water pond. The area should be wet enough that it has a slight shine, but you do not want puddles.

Apply color while the surface is still shiny to the upper bank area. At this stage you are creating a foundation for the detail that you will add later in the painting. Start by picking up diluted Indigo, which could have a hint of Burnt Umber added, on the 1-1/2 inch background brush. Make long horizontal strokes, apply the neutral color down toward the waterline.

Think about painting the rocks irregular shapes, colors and values. Pick up more diluted pigment on mostly the point of the angular brush. Use mixtures of Burnt Umber, Indigo, Burnt Sienna and hints of Country Brick. Form the rock shapes with the point of the brush towards the top of the paper and the shorter side towards the water. The color that diffuses into the water will work as a reflection. The diffused appearance of the rocks will give a softening effect and distant look.

You could add a few dabs of Hookers Green at the base of some of the rocks to create grass, vary the size, height and value. Dab over the rocks with a clean damp sponge for texture.

TOP WATER AREA

You most likely will need to re-wet the top water area. Be sure you have a clean brush as you apply a wash of water, as it is very easy to accidently pick up unwanted color from a dirty paper towel. Dilute the colors and mix them slightly, letting the pre-wet paper work for you, allow the pigment to flow together and mingle rather than become overworked and blend to one hue and value

It is helpful if you work at an angle. The travel table is an excellent support. When you pre-wet the paper and apply hints of pigment at the banks edge, they will dilute down beautifully. Pull some of the pigment back up into the rocks as well as pulling it into the water. Use variations of Country Brick, Burnt Umber and Indigo.

ROCKS

Before you start the rocks once again wet the area, and wet the area where you plan to paint the falls. As you paint the rock shapes, think of irregular patterns. Be careful not to repeat the size, shape and color.

Pick up more pigment on the point of the angular brush. Use variations of diluted Indigo, Burnt Umber, hints of Burnt Sienna and Country Brick. Plan the falls area as you paint the rocks. Dab with a clean damp sponge over the wet rocks to give a more textured appearance.

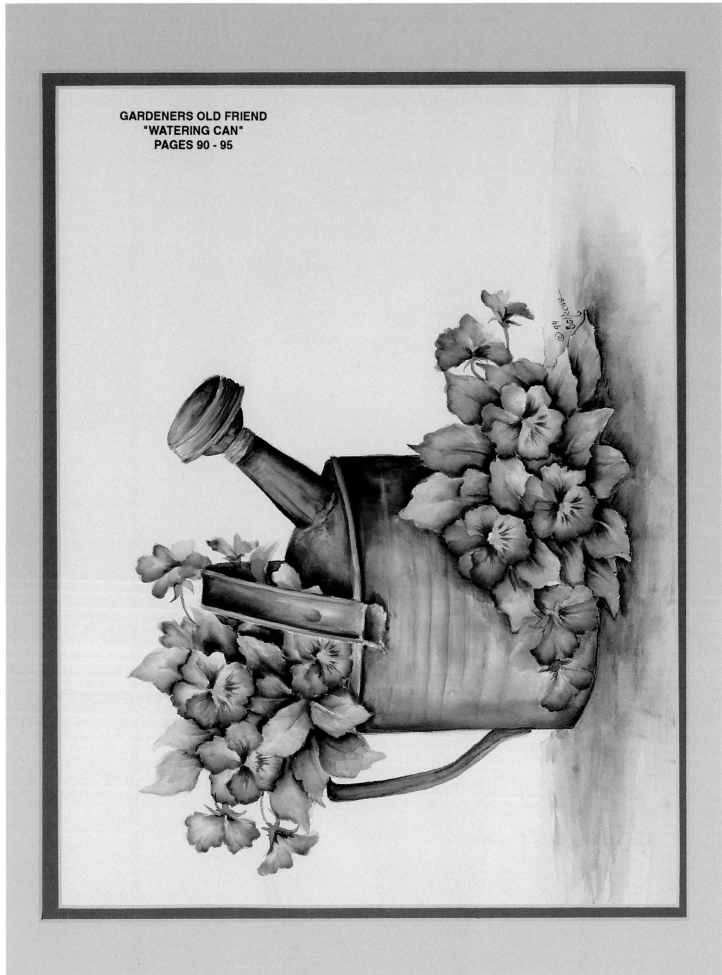

USE INSTRUCTIONS FOR
PANSIES IN,
GARDENER'S OLD FRIEND
"WATERING CAN"
PAGES 90 - 95

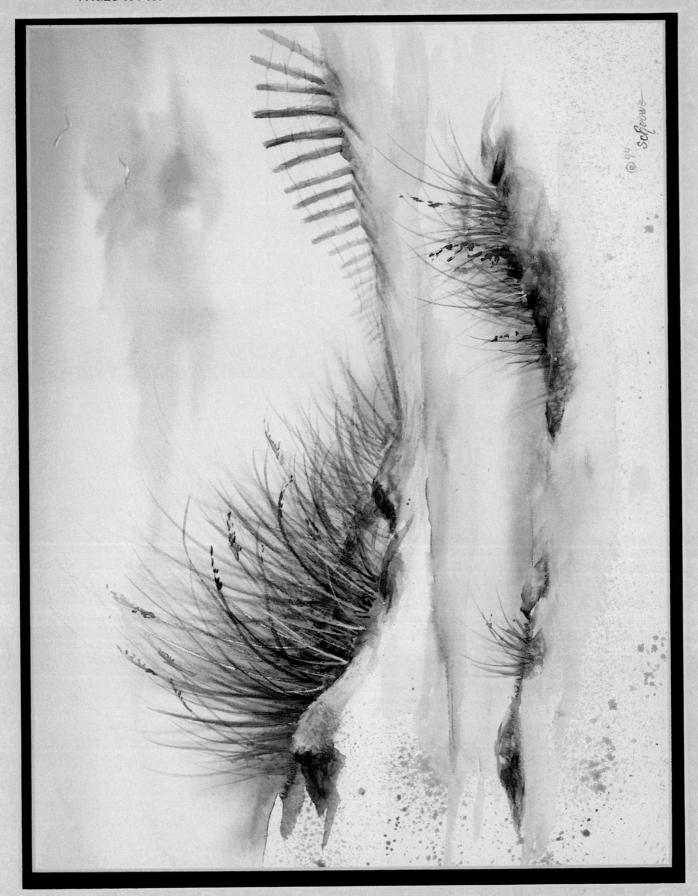

There is beautiful bright green moss that grows in our area, dab on a few mossy areas with Spring Green. If you uncomfortable with the moss, it's your painting, so leave it out.

WATERFALLS

The brush direction is of great importance when creating the appearance of water dancing down the rocks. You can always come back and add more pigment. Allow some of the soft edge to remain on the large rock in the center of the stream. It will then appear as though a sheer amount of water is coming over the rocks.

Apply pigment starting just above the top of the splash. Use a 1/2 inch angular shader pulling upward, lifting up on the pressure. The wax resist should repel the pigment making it easy for jets of water to appear. Use variations of Turquoise Deep with hints of Indigo and Ultramarine Blue. Use very diluted mixtures to lighten towards the middle and top of the falls.

On the bottom of the splash there will be shadow color created by the splash. Make sure you create a really irregular pattern dabbing up and down with the point of the angular shader. Use the same diluted variations as applied in the falls on the splash. Should for some reason you did not apply enough resist stick and color is appearing in an undesired place, first try lifting it off with a damp brush. If you lost the white and just can't get it back tap on some Chinese White.

TEXTURING ROCKS

Come back and blot the rocks after you have dampened them add a variety of color to create texture. Placing diluted pigment in a spray bottle, spray to create texture or appearance of small rocks Be careful to cover areas, that you do not want painted were you use the sprayer. Tap on some colors using a damp sponge.

GRASS AND MOSS

Look at the rock placement you have created and pull up blades of grass lifting gently as you swing the brush upward. Use a foliage brush with mixtures of Indigo, Hunters Green and Spring Green. Tap these variations at the base of the blades to create moss. As you apply single blades of grass use a liner, vary height and space. Be careful they don't all come from the same spot like a carrot. Pull and tap a few leafy twigs.

LOWER WATER AREA

The lower water area should be pre-wet with a 1-1/2 inch brush. Having the board at an angle will help as the water diffuse downward. Allow the pigment to mingle but don't overwork the area and blend the colors into one hue. As you paint the reflections, look at the area above and apply those colors on the angular shader. Think about the rock and the grass reflections as you paint.

The photo of this painting shows a lot of light area. Before you add a lot of color in the water areas on the large painting, try doing a smaller sample. Sometimes alterations look more eye appealing and sometimes you'll be glad you did these on small test paper.

TWIGS

Adding twigs gives a very natural appearance. You can add as few or as many twigs as you want. Use a liner with Burnt Umber.

FINISHING

Stand back from your painting and take a fresh look. Don't forget to dab these areas up and down when creating texture.

You can place a soft paper towel over the waxed area and then lightly go over the covered area to lift excess wax.

Enjoy this fun technique on other paintings.

"WATERFALL SPLASH"

SUSAN SCHEEWE WATERCOLORS
Indigo
Burnt Umber
Country Brick
Burnt Sienna
Hunters Green
Turquoise Deep
Hunters Green

BRUSHES
Series S8028, 1-1/2 Inch Background Shader

Resist Stick
140 or 300 lb. Cold Press Paper
Watercolor Resist Stick
Greeting Card

This is an easy design to extend into a long horizontal painting.
Think about the waterfall as you plan your design.

DAY AT THE BEACH

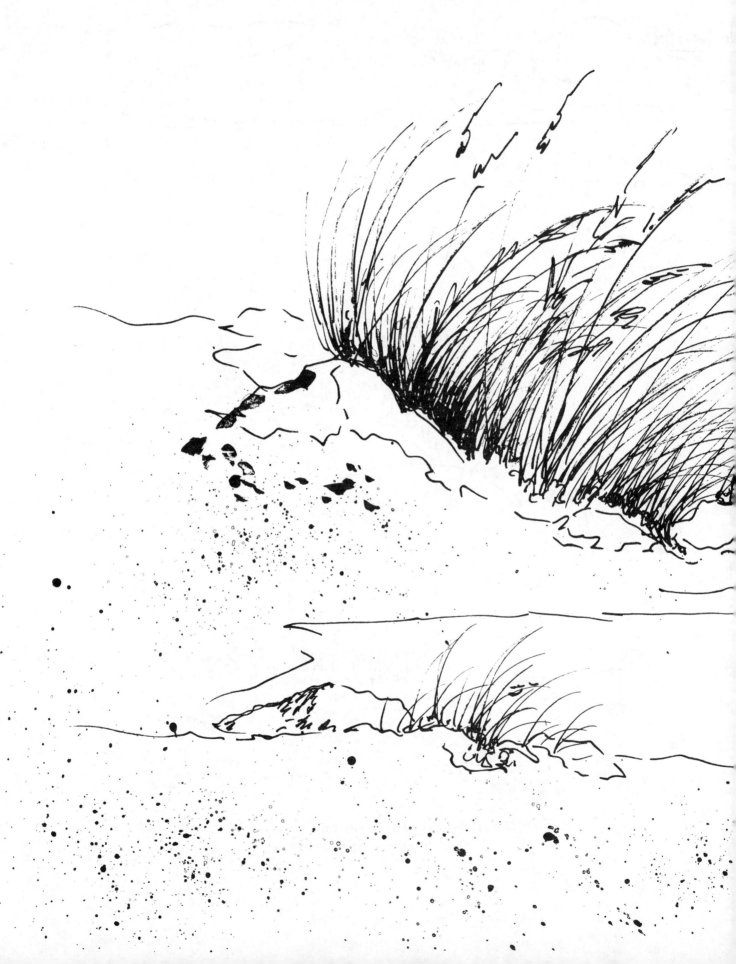

Going on vacation to the beach?

Take a large stack of greeting cards along with your paints and brushes to create wonderful cards to send to special family friends. Let everyone including the children paint cards.
A wonderful activity for those sometimes unexpected rainy days as well as creating special memories to share.

© 1994
Suzanne
Brown

DAY AT THE BEACH

SUSAN SCHEEWE WATERCOLORS
Turquoise Deep
Cobalt Blue (Optional)
Indigo
Raw Sienna
Burnt Sienna
Violet (Optional)

BRUSHES
Series S8028, Size 1-1/2 Inch Angular
Series S8017, Size 1 Liner

Sponge
Spray Bottle

This painting can easily be adapted to many sizes, shapes and colors. The color Indigo, seems to magically match and recreate the blue gray tones of a foggy day at the beach. I'm familiar with those days living at the Oregon Coast for a couple of years.

The shifting sand dunes have their own beautiful changes. This is a fun and easy painting. You might collect some sea shells and glue them to the mat to make a unique and interesting frame.

A perfect painting for a rainy day at the coast or, if you are unable to get away to the beach this painting can be a wonderful escape. Build a nice fire, turn on some music, gather the children around the table and everyone can paint cards to send home. The paints and brushes are easy to pack in the suitcase and have ready to reach. Don't forget to take the cards and stamps. Think about adding sea gulls, sea shells or a float in the painting. Have fun making many changes.

Make a sketch lightly with a pencil on the surface.

SKY

Pre-wet the sky area coming down to the horizon line using a 1-1/2 inch angular background brush. Make sure the paper is really wet. This wet into wet technique will make blending far easier. Pick up diluted Turquoise Deep and apply towards the top of the sky. Add more water to lighten the value as you work toward the horizon.

You can easily lift off color by patting the surface with a soft dry paper towel or a clean, almost dry brush or a sponge to make clouds. All these items are very helpful painting tools. Next you can add clouds by dabbing the wet surface with more pigment on a brush or dab on a little pigment with a sponge. Adding hints of Indigo with a touch of Cobalt Blue is pretty.

The wet surface will a create soft diffused edge. It is far easier to paint clouds using watercolors than it is with acrylic or oils.

Re-wet the area along the horizon line upward. As you look at your horizon line do not paint a straight line as it can appear very stiff, think of painting an uneven interesting line. You could lightly spray on clean water to dampen the area or add clean water with a brush.

GRASS AREA

Pick up a little Raw Sienna and Indigo on the brush. Dab a lot of pigment at the horizon line to create an irregular pattern that dabs up like ground foliage. Quickly turn your brush around to use the chiseled end of the plastic handle to scrape the wet surface, lifting from the color applied upward with a curving motion. The most common mistake is not pulling enough blades quickly, the second is sometimes making them too stiff and uniform. When the surface is real wet the pigment will flow into the groove. As the paper starts to dry you can lift the pigment and scrape it back exposing a lighter portion of the paper. The plastic beveled handle brushes work wonderfully as they don't break, the wooden handles often split and wear down.

Once the surface has dried you cannot scrape the pigment, but you can apply it with a liner to create delicate grass blades and sea oats. Use diluted variations of color to create these blades. Tap a little at the end of a few blades to create the appearance of oats. Check to see if you have varied the height.

WATER AREA

Painting a tide pool or puddle after a rain storm is easy. Try not to make a perfectly round circle but create an interesting shape. Pre-wet this area with a clean wet brush. Most often open water areas will reflect the sky. Apply diluted Turquoise Deep towards the bottom of the water. Pick up the paper and allow the pigment to run towards the horizon, but be careful to not create a puddle of water as this will streak down the paper as you tilt it.

If you applied other colors in the sky you will want to add these to the water area as the water generally reflects the sky color. If you have painted grass blades near the water you might consider painting a reflection.

It is helpful to lightly stroke across with a damp brush to give the illusion of movement. If you brush a lot you'll create a solid color. Don't over work this area.

SAND AND SPLATTER

It is fun to splatter the surface but it is important to cover areas that you want to protect from stray flecks with a clean paper towel.

You will first want to apply a diluted wash of Raw Sienna and a hint of Indigo in the sand area using the 3/4 angular. Pre-wet this area if you are doing a large painting, on a small painting it wouldn't be necessary.

Cover the sky area with a soft clean paper towel or paper, you will also want to protect your water area. Pick up a lot of water and pigment, test on a scrap paper first. Place your finger under the fibers and pull your finger upward as you push the brush down, splattering the surface. You can use several values of the same color or use a variation of mixtures. If the brush isn't wet enough you'll get a very fine splatter, if the brush is too wet it will have big blops (technical term). Check it on a test paper.

SUSAN SCHEEWE WATERCOLOR SEMINAR

Join in the excitement of learning more about watercolors. You can take a week of watercolor training for your painting pleasure or you can become a Susan Scheewe Certified Instructor.

Classes are held in Portland, Oregon and across the United States. Write for information and schedules.

PRIMARY LEVEL SEMINAR - Is an introduction to watercolors. Emphasis will be on understanding the many techniques used in completing watercolor painting. The importance of understanding the variety of surfaces will be included as painted samples are being completed. As the participants work on samples for their notebook they will learn the skills which will be applied to class paintings which will be completed during the training session.

SECONDARY LEVEL SEMINAR - This session will emphasize techniques and more advance projects. Projects will be completed for make-it take-it promotions, demonstrations, and teaching skills. Learning skills of how to make corrections as you do more advance paintings.

CERTIFICATION LEVEL is the exciting step to complete the certification series. More advanced projects will be painted. Sharpening the teaching skills will be stressed. A guest speaker from the Martin/F. Weber Co. or Scheewe Publications will come to the seminar to discuss promotion, class set-up, product sourcing and other valuable information for Scheewe Instructors.

WATERCOLOR BOOKS

Vol. 20	"Simply Country Watercolors" by Susan Scheewe Brown	257	$9.50	___
Vol. 21	"Simply Watercolor" by Susan Scheewe Brown.....T.V. Book	260	$11.95	___
Vol. 22	"Watercolor For Everyone" by Susan Scheewe Brown.....T.V. Book	276	$11.95	___
Vol. 23	"Watercolor Step by Step" by Susan Scheewe Brown.....T.V. Book	294	$11.95	___
Vol. 24	"Introduction to Watercolor" by Susan Scheewe Brown.....T.V. Book	314	$11.95	___
Vol. 25	"Watercolors Anyone Can Paint" by Susan Scheewe Brown...T.V. Book	325	$11.95	___
*NEW Vol. 26	"Watercolor - The Garden Scene" by Susan Scheewe Brown... T.V. Book	341	$11.95	___
Vol. 4	"Enjoy Watercolor" by Ellie Cook	210	$7.50	___
Vol. 6	"Watercolor Memories" by Ellie Cook	246	$9.50	___
Vol. 7	"My Favorite Things In Watercolor" by Ellie Cook	293	$9.50	___
Vol. 3	"Watercolor Made Easy 3" by Kathy George	301	$9.50	___
Vol. 1	"The Way I Started" by Gary Hawk	120	$6.00	___
Vol. 2	"Anyone Can Watercolor" by Ken Johnson	118	$6.50	___
Vol. 1	"Watercolor Fun & Easy" by Beverly Kaiser	243	$7.50	___
Vol. 1	"Flowers, Ribbon and Lace in Watercolor" by Linda McCulloch	280	$9.50	___

PEN & INK BOOKS / COLORED PENCIL BOOKS

Vol. 6	"Journey of Memories" by Claudia Nice	166	$6.50	___
Vol. 7	"Scenes from Seasons Past" by Claudia Nice	183	$9.50	___
Vol. 8	"Taste of Summer" by Claudia Nice	223	$9.50	___
Vol. 9	"Familiar Faces" by Claudia Nice	284	$9.50	___
Vol. 2	"Colored Pencil Made Easy" by Jane Wunder	242	$7.50	___
Vol. 3	"The Beauty of Colored Pencil and Ink Drawing" by Jane Wunder	259	$7.50	___

VIDEOS BY SUSAN SCHEEWE BROWN

"The Gift Of Painting Simply Watercolor" 60 Minutes	$24.95	___
"The Gift Of Painting" 90 Minutes	$24.95	___
"Paintings For The Holidays" 60 Minutes	$24.95	___
"Watercolor & Oil Do Mix" 60 Minutes	$24.95	___
"Watercolor Special Effects" 60 Minutes	$24.95	___

——— OILS BOOKS ———

Vol. 1	"His and Hers" by Susan Scheewe	101	$6.50	___	Vol. 3	"Winter Song" by Gloria Gaffney	271	$9.50
Vol. 6	"Brushed With Elegance" by Susan Scheewe	106	$9.50	___	Vol. 1	"Roses Are For Everyone" by Bill Huffaker	145	$9.50
Vol. 7	"Paint 'n Patch" by Susan Scheewe	107	$5.50	___	Vol. 3	"Nature's Beauty" by Bill Huffaker	177	$6.50
Vol. 11	"I Love To Paint" by Susan Scheewe	111	$9.50	___	Vol. 1	"Copper, Silver, Brass & Glass" by Susan Jenkins	211	$6.50
Vol. 14	"Enjoy Painting Animals" by Susan Scheewe	114	$9.50	___	Vol. 1	"In Full Bloom" by Susan Jenkins	313	$9.50
Vol. 17	"Countryside Reflections" by Susan Scheewe	161	$6.50	___	Vol. 1	"Backroads of My Memory" by Geri Kisner	225	$9.50
Vol. 19	"Gift Of Painting" by Susan Scheewe O/AC/WC	230	$9.50	___	Vol. 2	"Backroads of My Memory" by Geri Kisner	245	$9.50
Vol. 1	"Western Images" by Becky Anthony	186	$6.50	___	Vol. 1	"Ducks and Geese" by Jean Lyles	172	$6.50
Vol. 3	"Fantasy Flowers II" by Georgia Bartlett	129	$6.50	___	Vol. 1	"Raining Cats & Dogs" by Todd Mallett	304	$9.50
Vol. 5	"Soft Petals" by Georgia Bartlett	171	$6.50	___	Vol. 1	"Pathway To Painting" by Lee McGowan	281	$9.50
Vol. 6	"Painting Fantasy Flowers" by Georgia Bartlett	215	$7.50	___	Vol. 2	"Another Path To Follow" by Lee McGowen	328	$9.50
Vol. 7	"Flowers" by Georgia Bartlett	290	$9.50	___	Vol. 1	"Bitterroot Backroads" by Glenice Moore	330	$9.50
Vol. 8	"Petals" by Georgia Bartlett	317	$9.50	___	Vol. 2	"Bitterroot Backroads 2" by Glenice Moore....*NEW	340	$9.50
Vol. 9	"Floral Medley" by Georgia Bartlett....*NEW	344	$9.50	___	Vol. 1	"Stepping Stones" by Judy Nutter	121	$6.50
Vol. 3	"Barnscapes & More" by Donna Bell	218	$9.50	___	Vol. 1	"Painting with Paulson" by Buck Paulson....*NEW	343	$11.95
Vol. 4	"Countryscapes" by Donna Bell	249	$9.50	___	Vol. 1	"Rustic Charms" by Sharon Rachal	175	$6.50
Vol. 5	"Painter to Painter" by Donna Bell	263	$9.50	___	Vol. 2	"Rustic Charms II" by Sharon Rachal	199	$6.50
Vol. 6	"Landscapes With Acrylics & Oil" by Donna Bell	282	$9.50	___	Vol. 3	"Rustic Charms III" by Sharon Rachal	217	$6.50
Vol. 1	"Natures Palette" by Carol Binford.....O/AC	248	$9.50	___	Vol. 4	"Rustic Charms IV" by Sharon Rachal	238	$7.50
Vol. 1	"Oil Painting The Easy Way" by Bill Blackman	219	$9.50	___	Vol. 5	"Rustic Charms V, Florals" by Sharon Rachal	261	$9.50
Vol. 2	"Oil Painting The Easy Way" by Bill Blackman ....*NEW	337	$9.50	___	Vol. 1	"Painting Flowers With Augie" by Augie Reis	152	$6.50
Vol. 1	"Mini Mini More" by Terri and Nancy Brown	150	$9.50	___	Vol. 2	"Painting Realism" by Judy Sleight	272	$9.50
Vol. 2	"Mini Mini More" by Terri and Nancy Brown	151	$9.50	___	Vol. 3	"Realistic Technique" by Judy Sleight....*NEW	341	$9.50
Vol. 4	"Heritage Trails" by Terri and Nancy Brown	169	$6.50	___	Vol. 1	"Soft & Misty Paintings" by Kathy Snider	204	$9.50
Vol. 6	"Garden Trails" by Terri and Nancy Brown	283	$9.50	___	Vol. 2	"Soft & Misty Paintings" by Kathy Snider	229	$9.50
Vol. 2	"Windows of My World" by Jackie Claflin	181	$9.50	___	Vol. 4	"Friends We've Known" by Gene Waggoner	187	$7.50
Vol. 3	"Windows of My World 3" by Jackie Claflin	303	$9.50	___	Vol. 5	"Friends Are Forever" by Gene Waggoner	231	$7.50
Vol. 4	"Expressions In Oil" by Delores Egger	239	$7.50	___	Vol. 1	"Fantasy Folk" by Don Weed	123	$6.50
Vol. 1	"Victorian Days" by Gloria Gaffney	240	$9.50	___	Vol. 2	"Painting The Clowns" by Don Weed	124	$6.50
Vol. 2	"Days of Heaven" by Gloria Gaffney	252	$9.50	___	Vol. 1	"Something Special For Everyone" by Mildred Yeiser	158	$6.50
					Vol. 2	"Something Special For Everyone" by Mildred Yeiser	178	$6.50
					Vol. 5	"Soft & Gentle Paintings" by Mildred Yeiser	268	$9.50

NAME _____

ADDRESS _____

CITY/STATE/ZIP _____

PH( ) _____

VISA _____

M/C _____

EXP. DATE _____

SHIPPING $ _____

SHIP TO _____

Susan Scheewe Publications Inc.

13435 N.E. Whitaker Way Portland, Or. 97230 PH (503) 254-9100 FAX (503) 252-9508